MY HUNTRESS

COLORING BOOK

I0483510

Original Pen & Ink Artwork by Brenda Potts

www.BooksByPotts.com

ACKNOWLEDGMENT

Many thanks to Alli and Adriana Armstrong

whose "GRACE, CAMO & LACE" lifestyle provided

inspiration for the drawings in this book.

www.gracecamoandlace.com

Cover photos courtesy of Armstrongs Outdoors

Background Cover Illustration by Larisa Vakhtine, Hemera Collection ThinkstockPhotos.com

ISBN 978-0-9883272-7-6

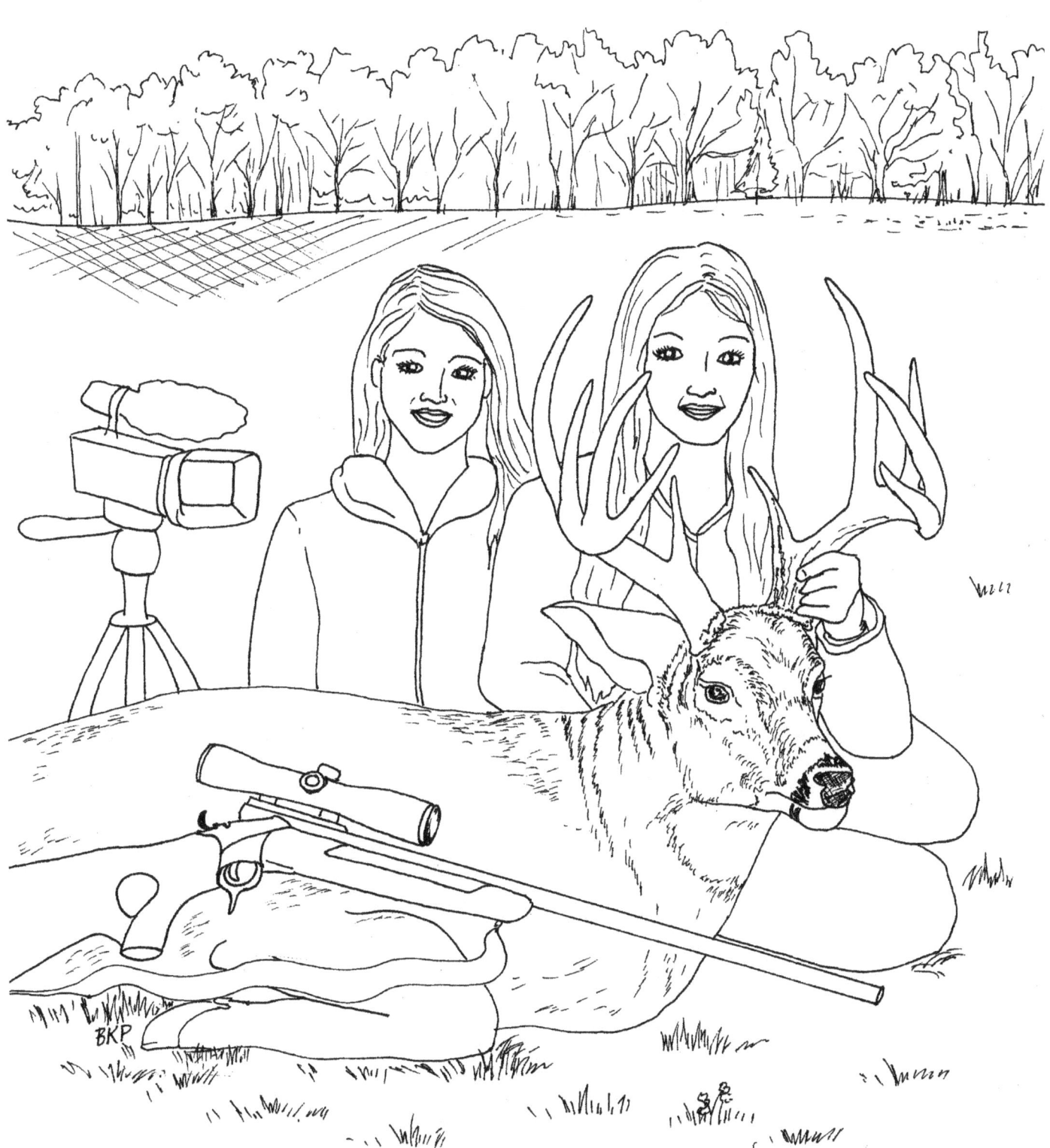

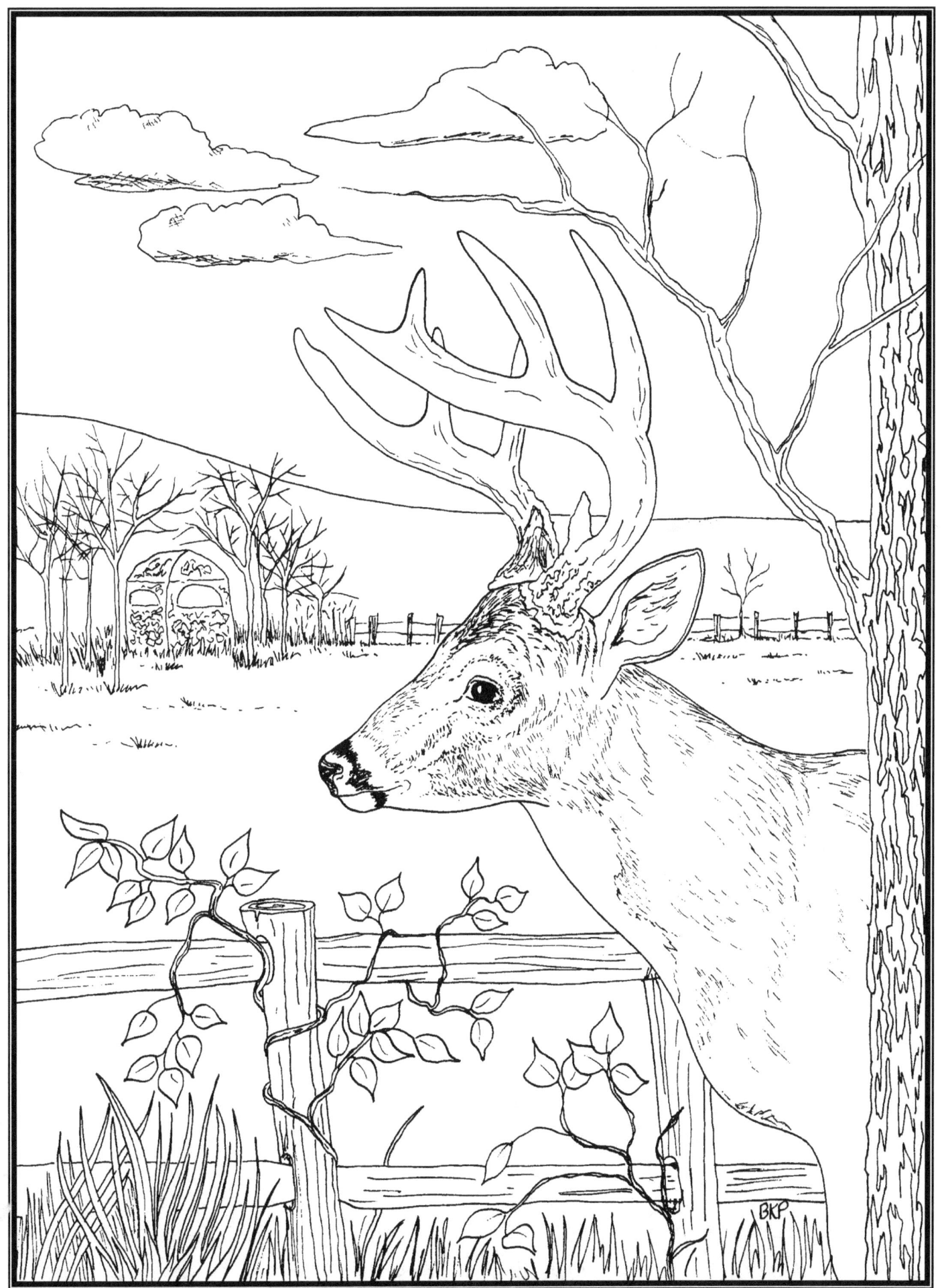

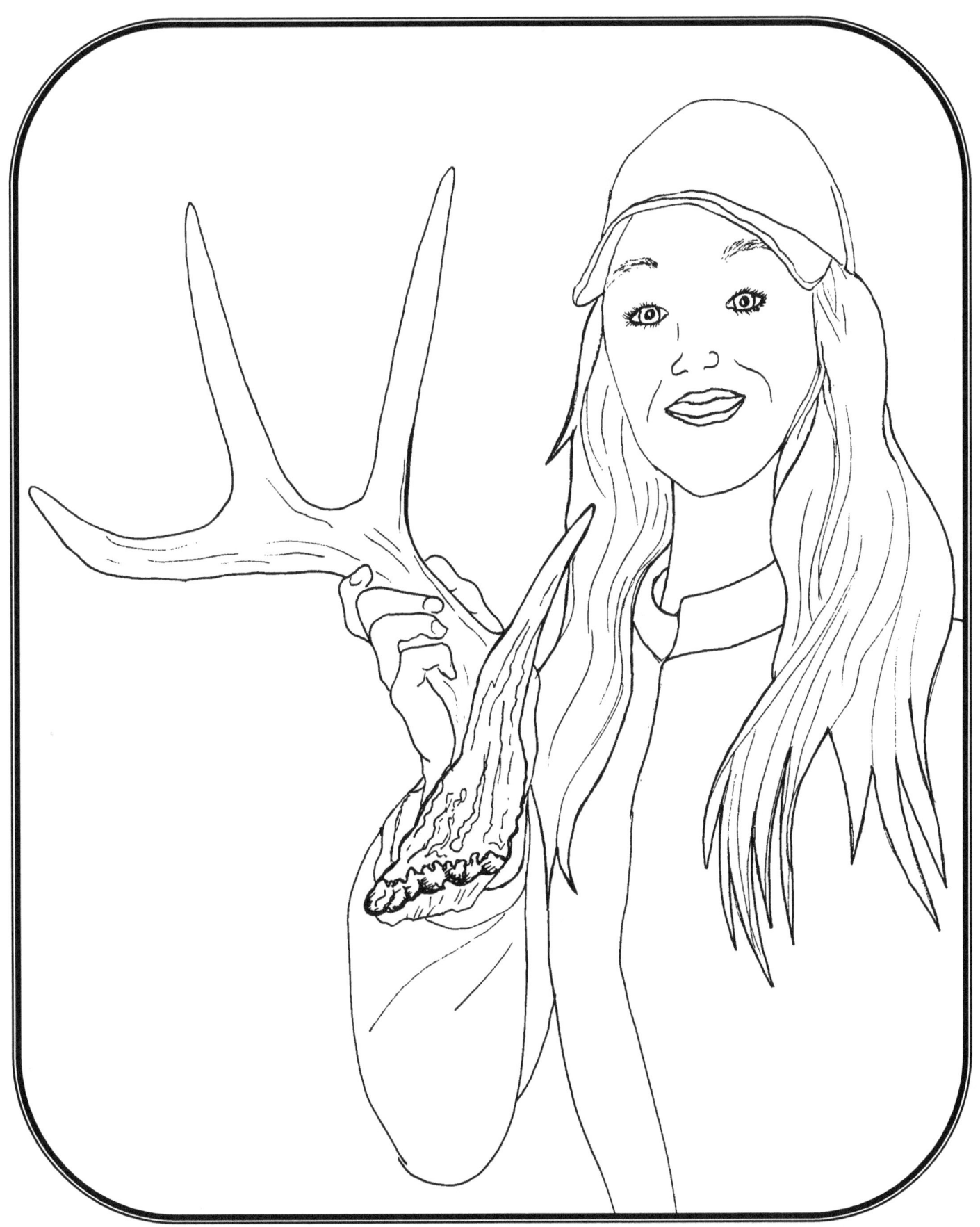

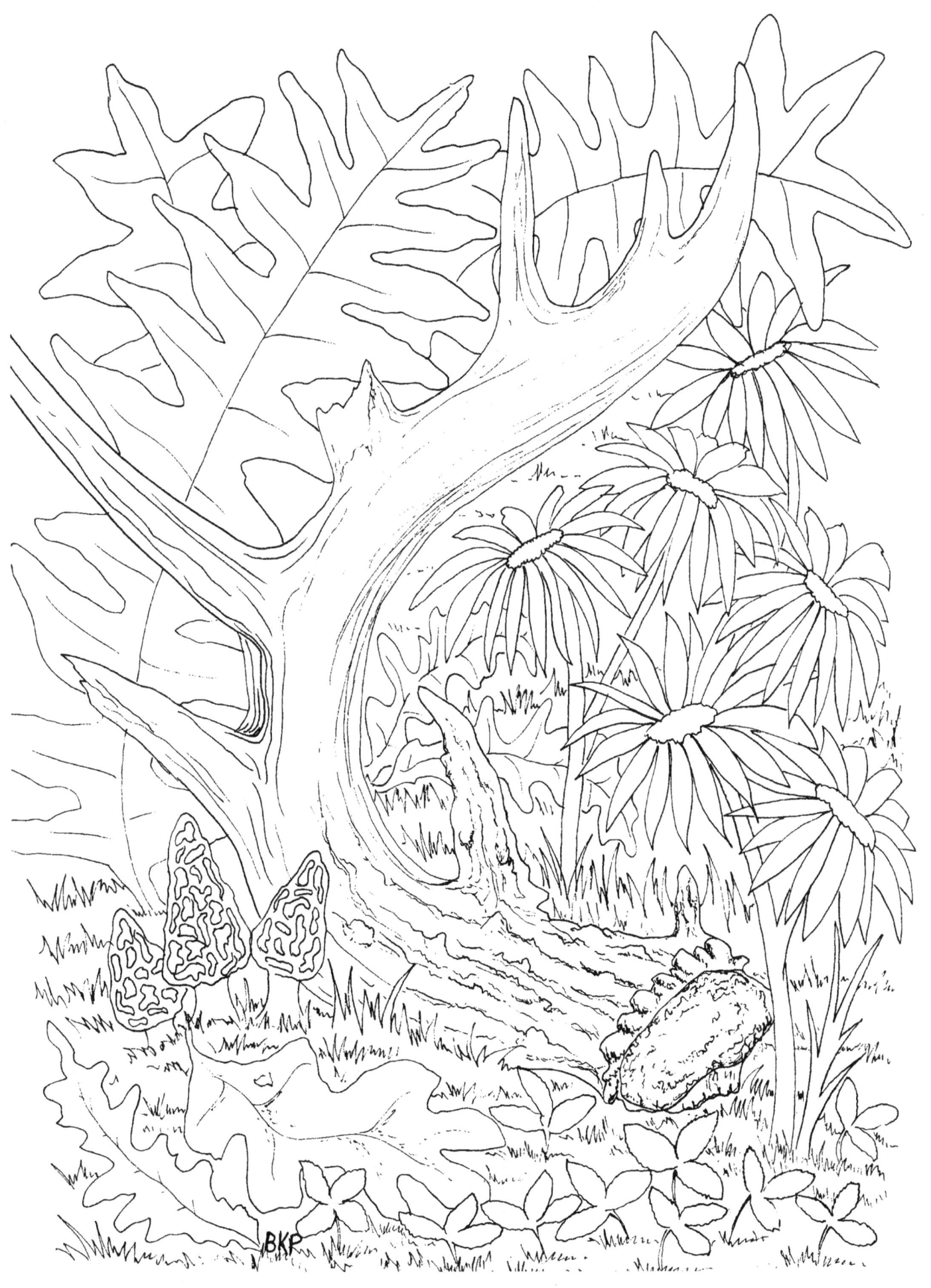

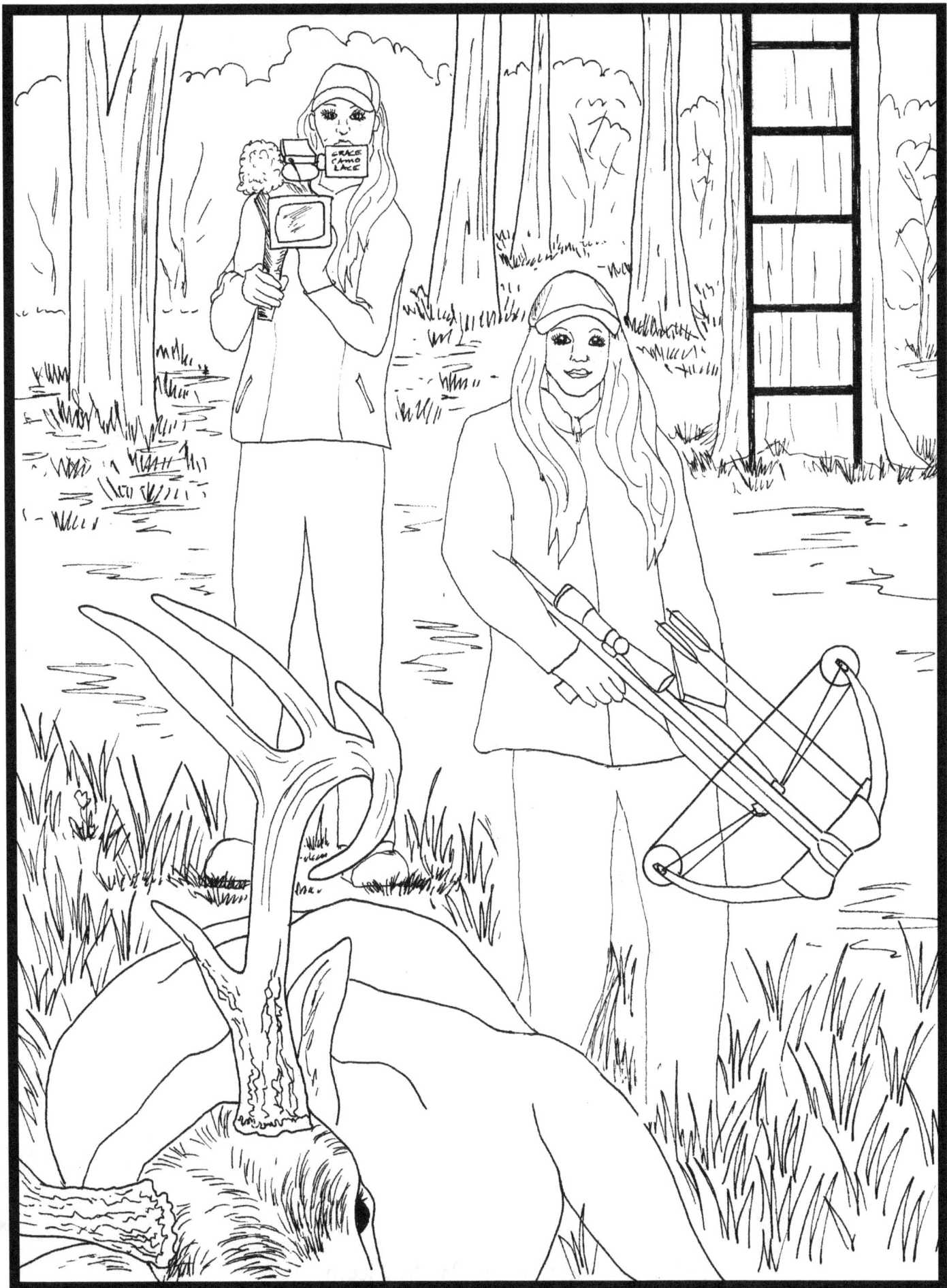

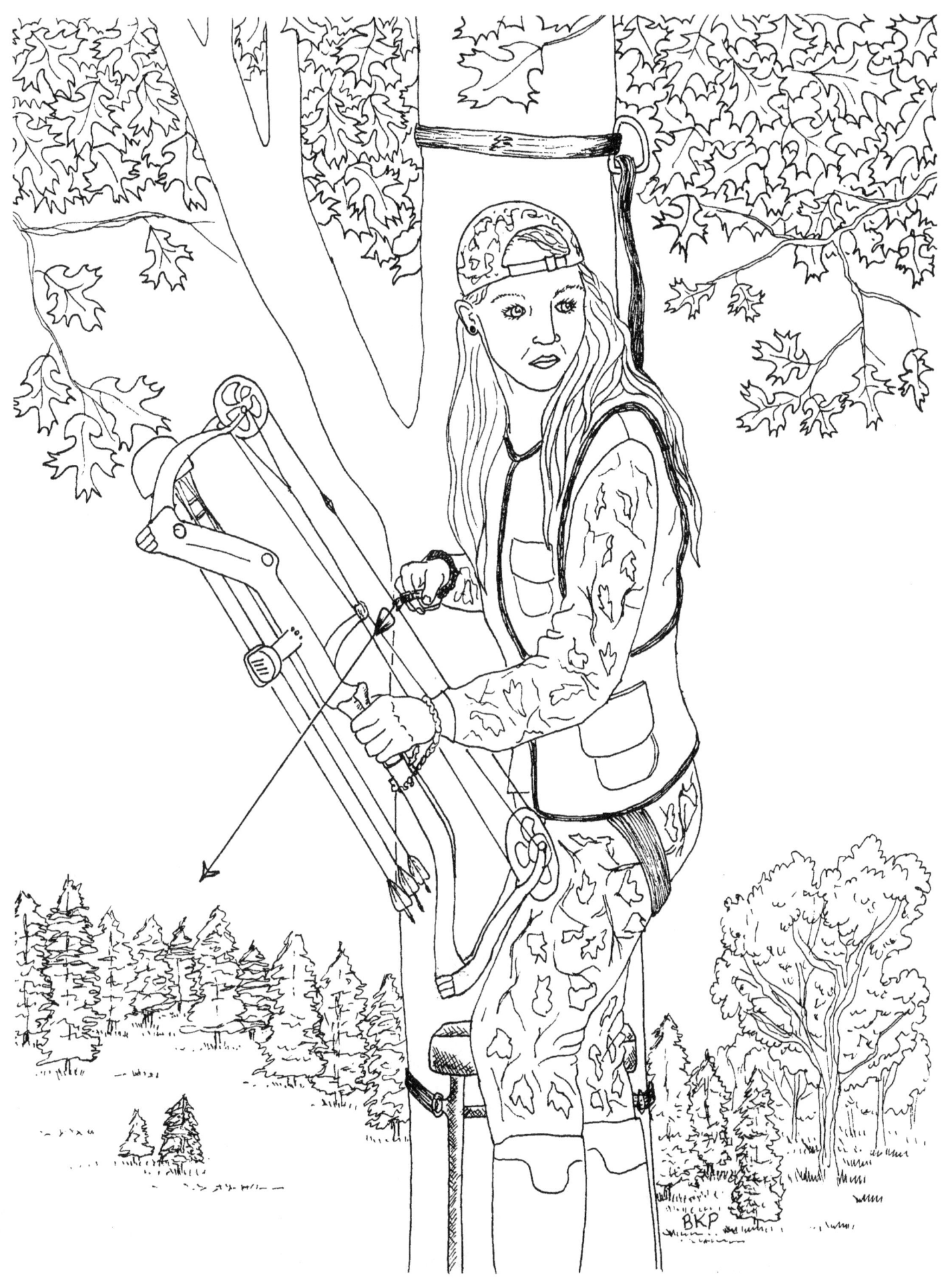

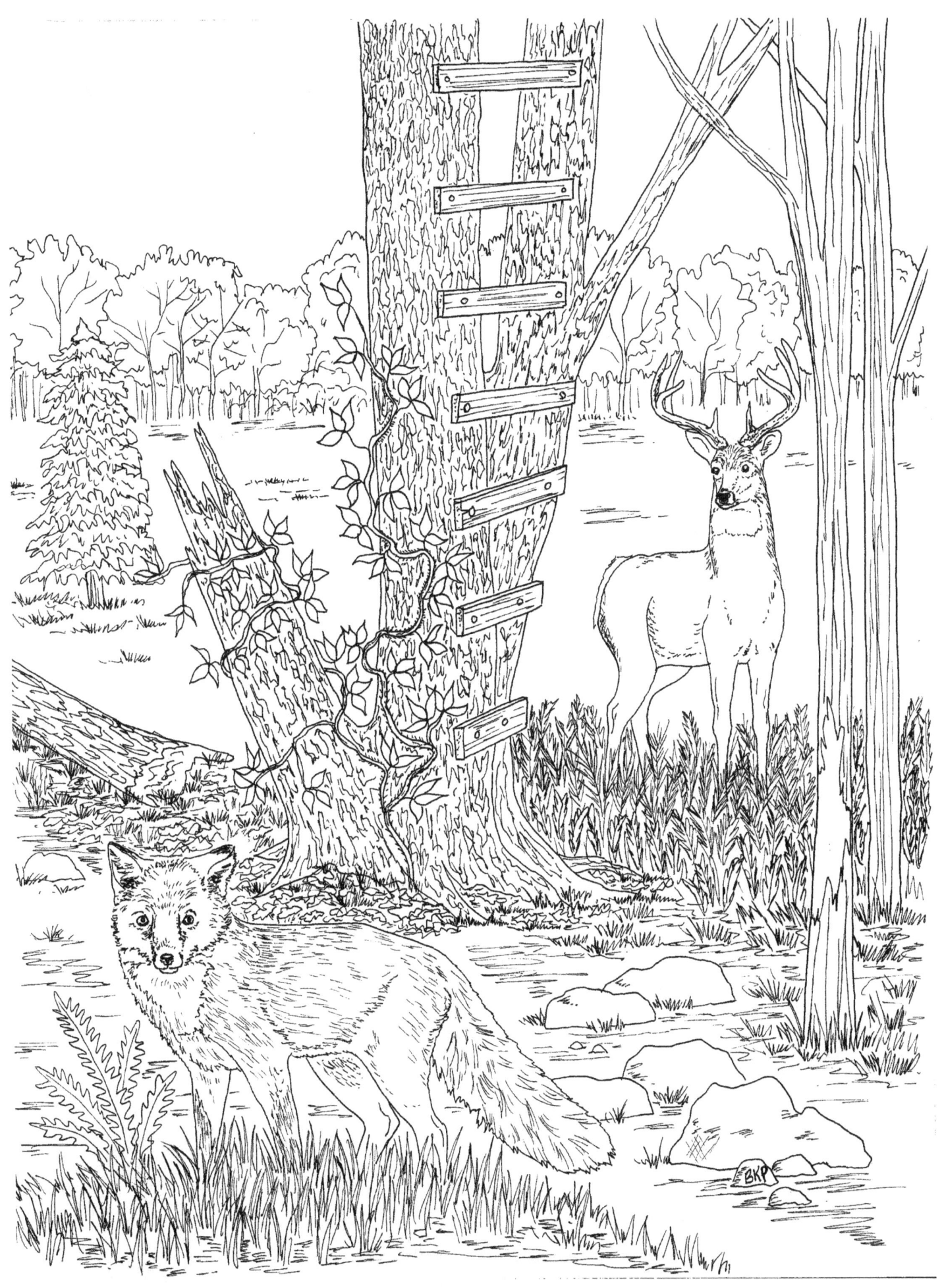

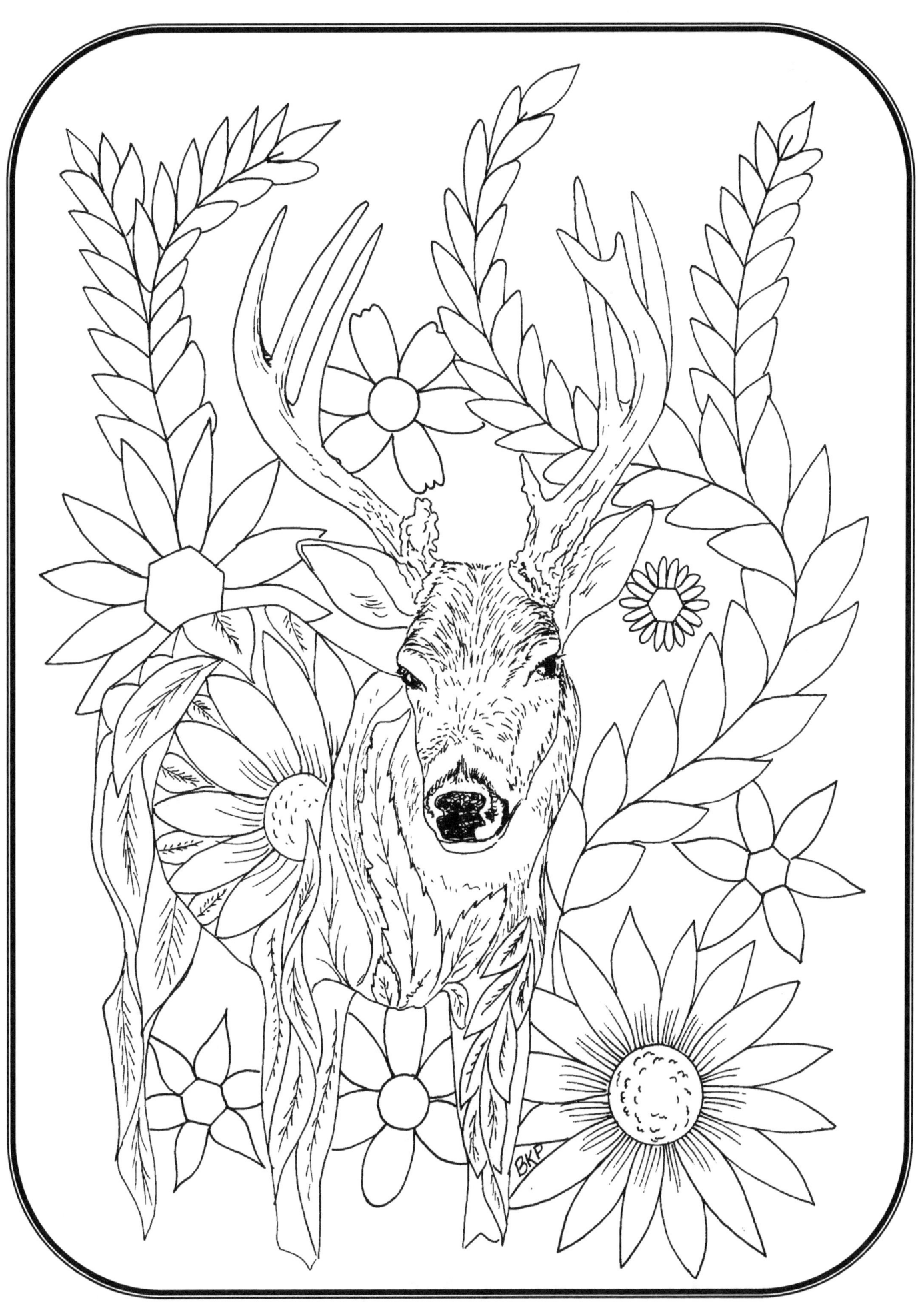

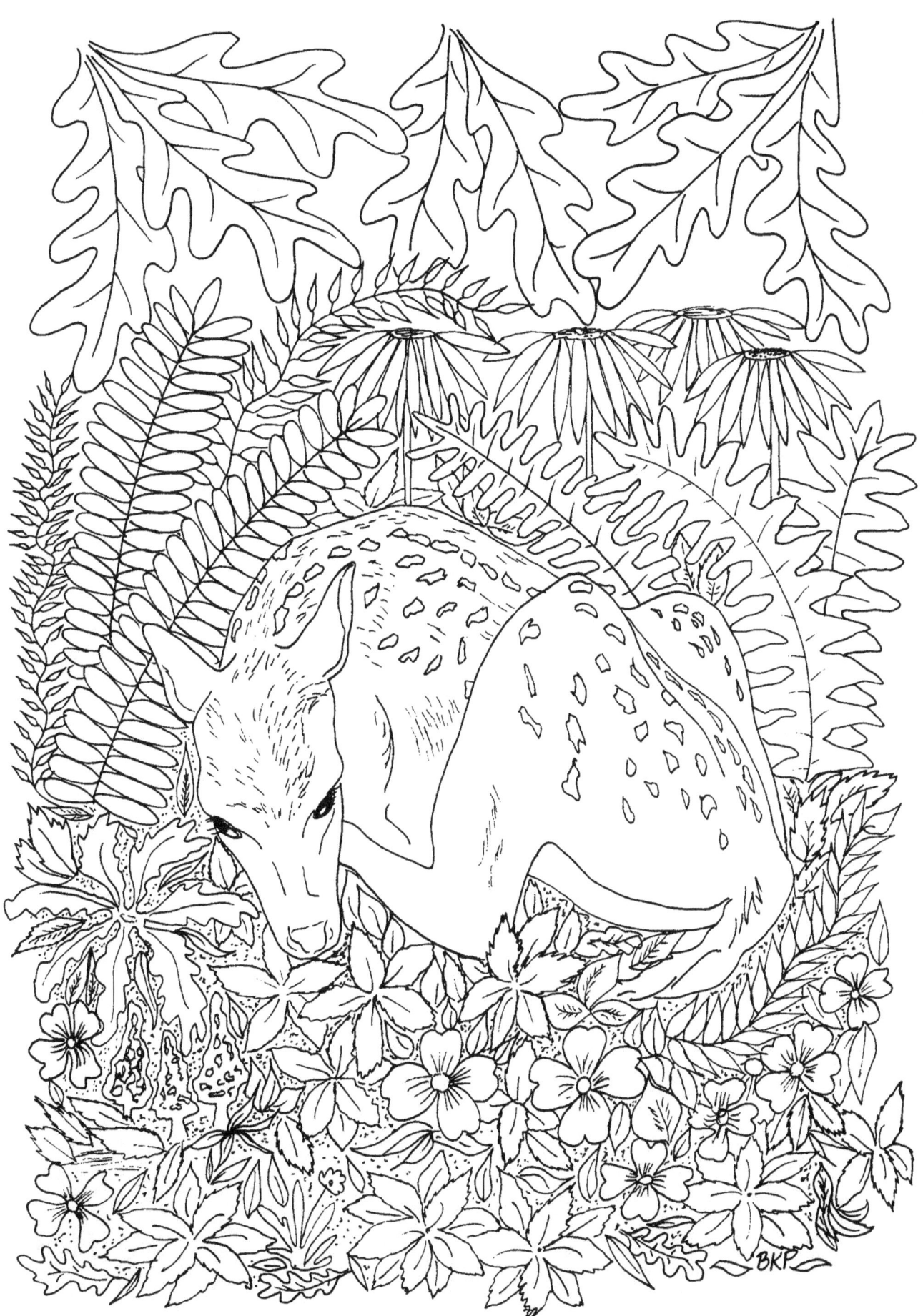

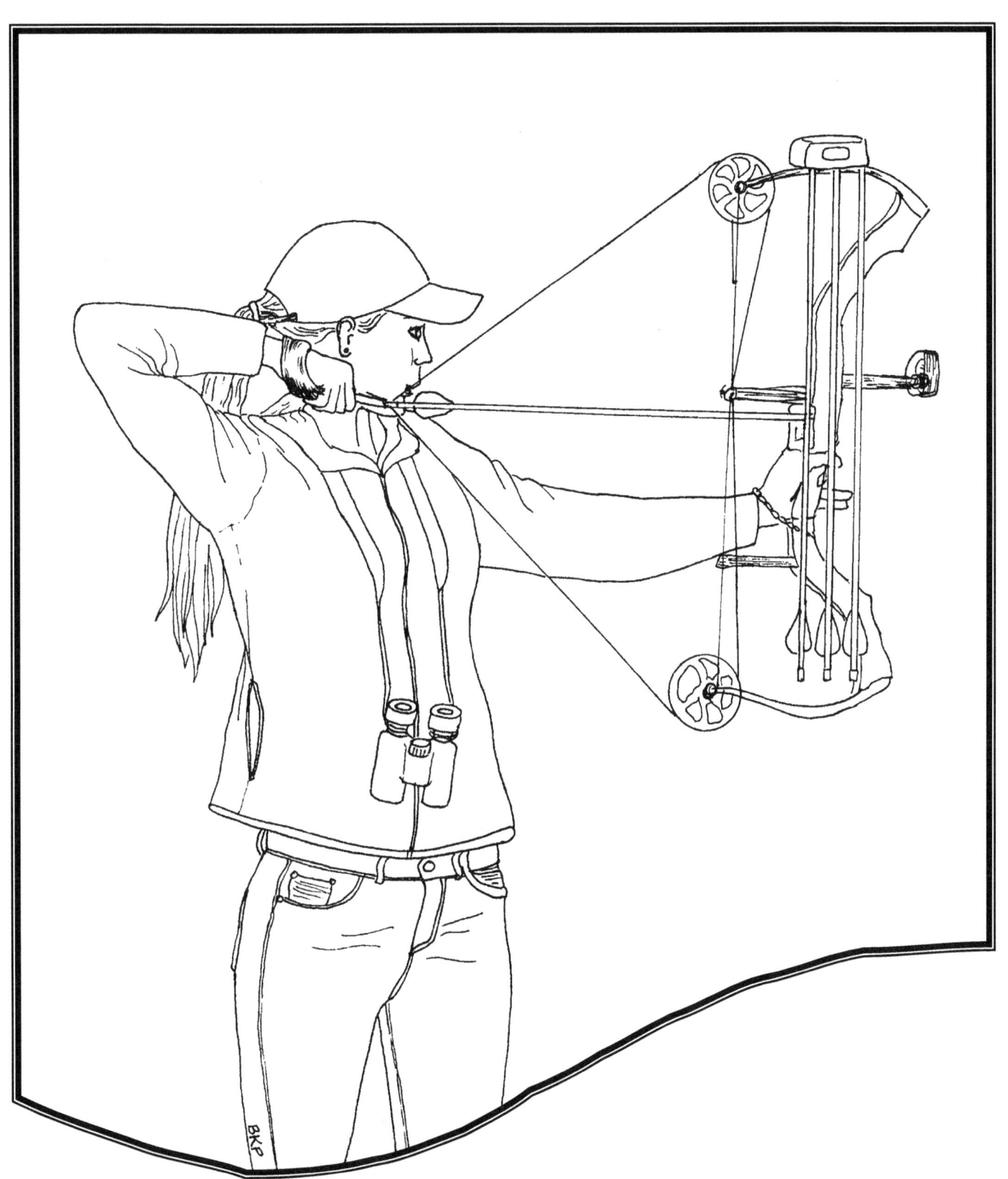

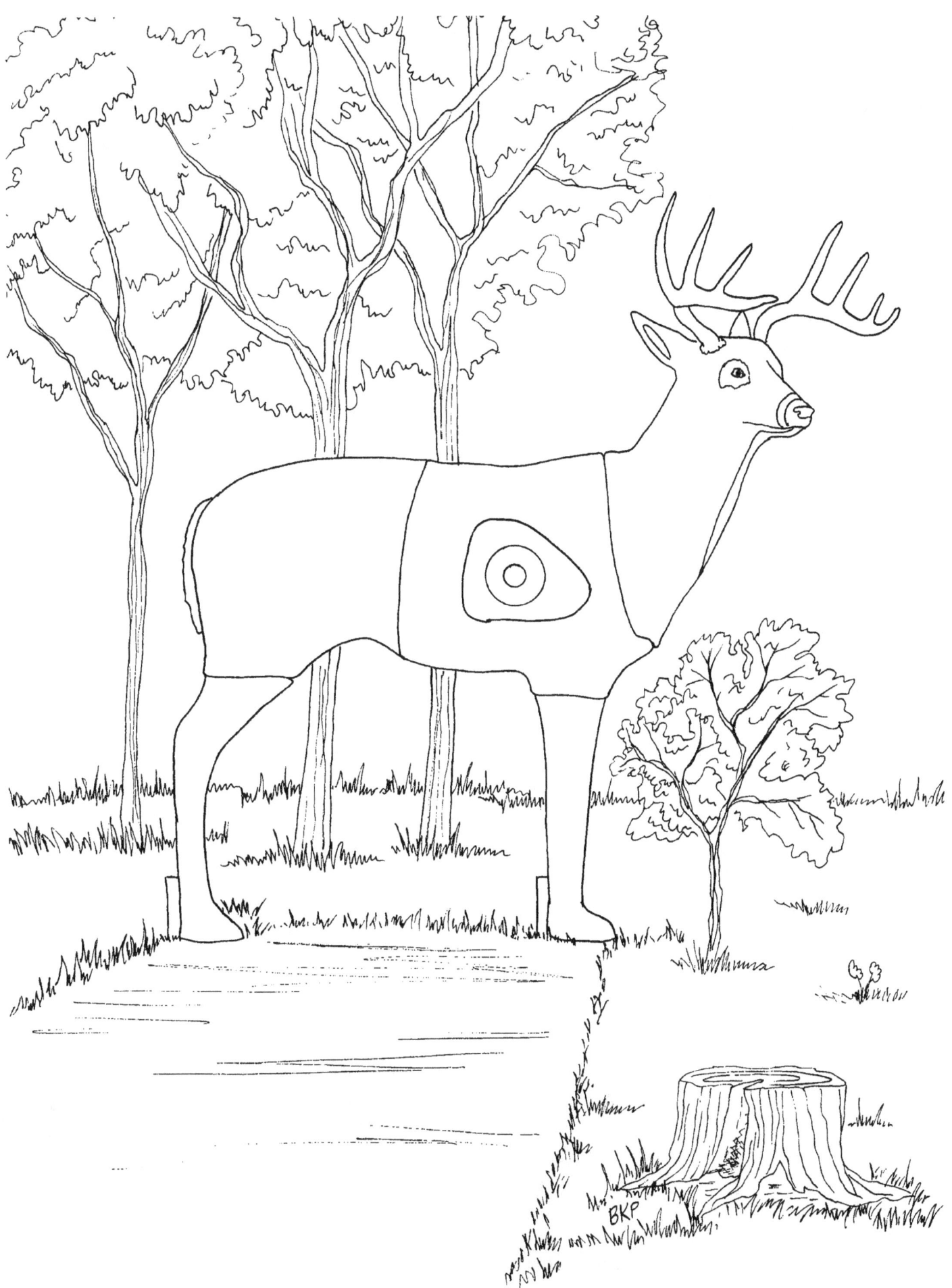

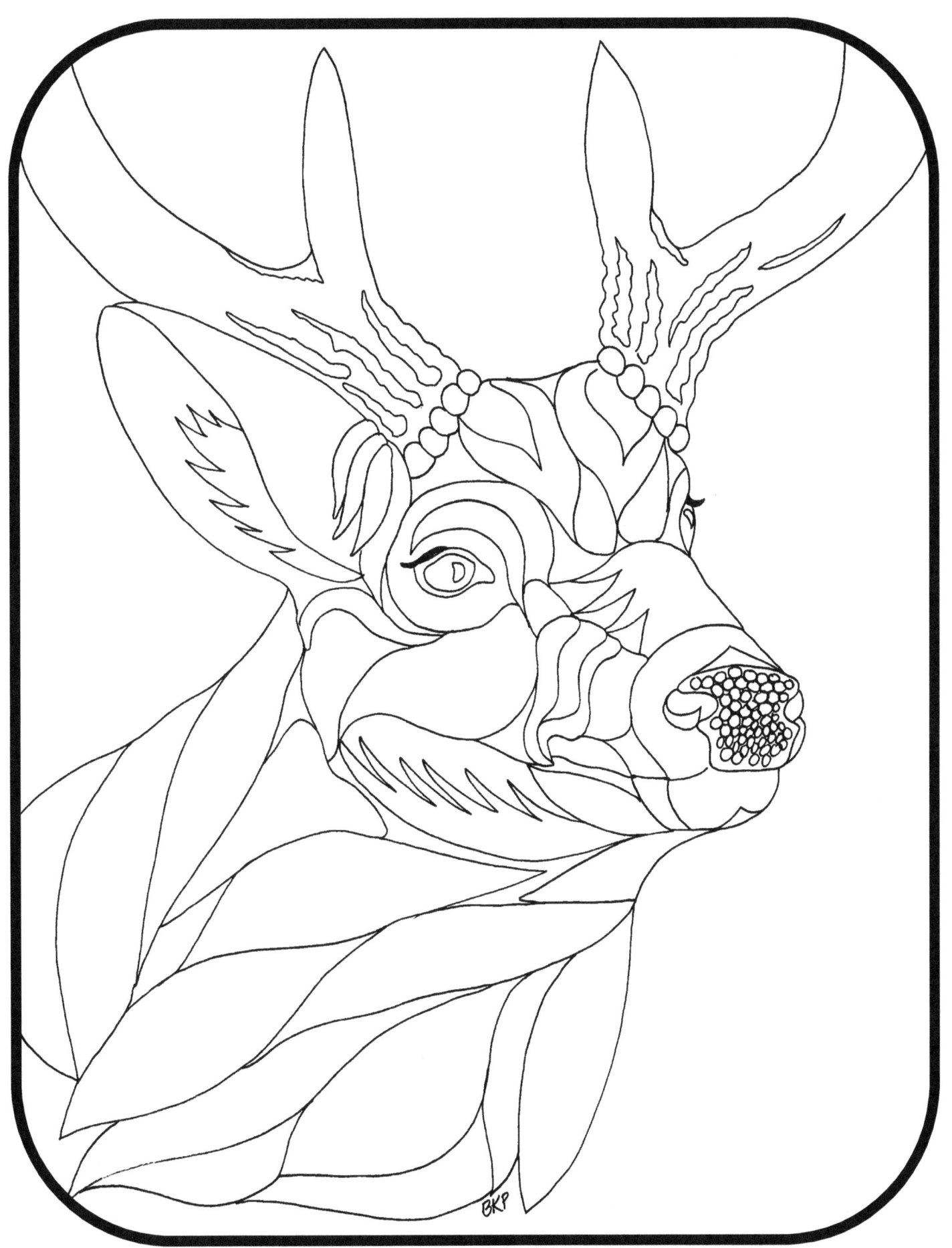

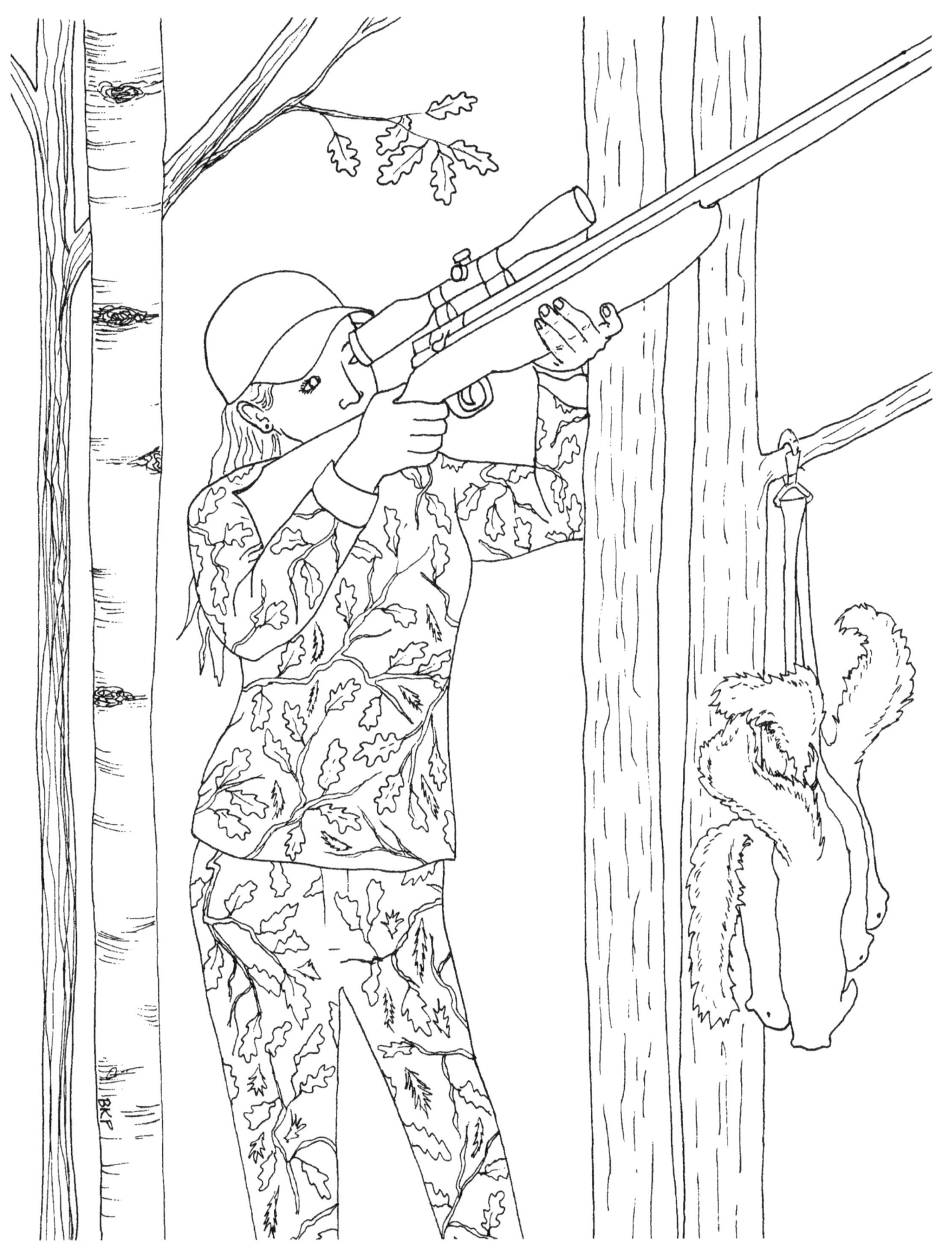

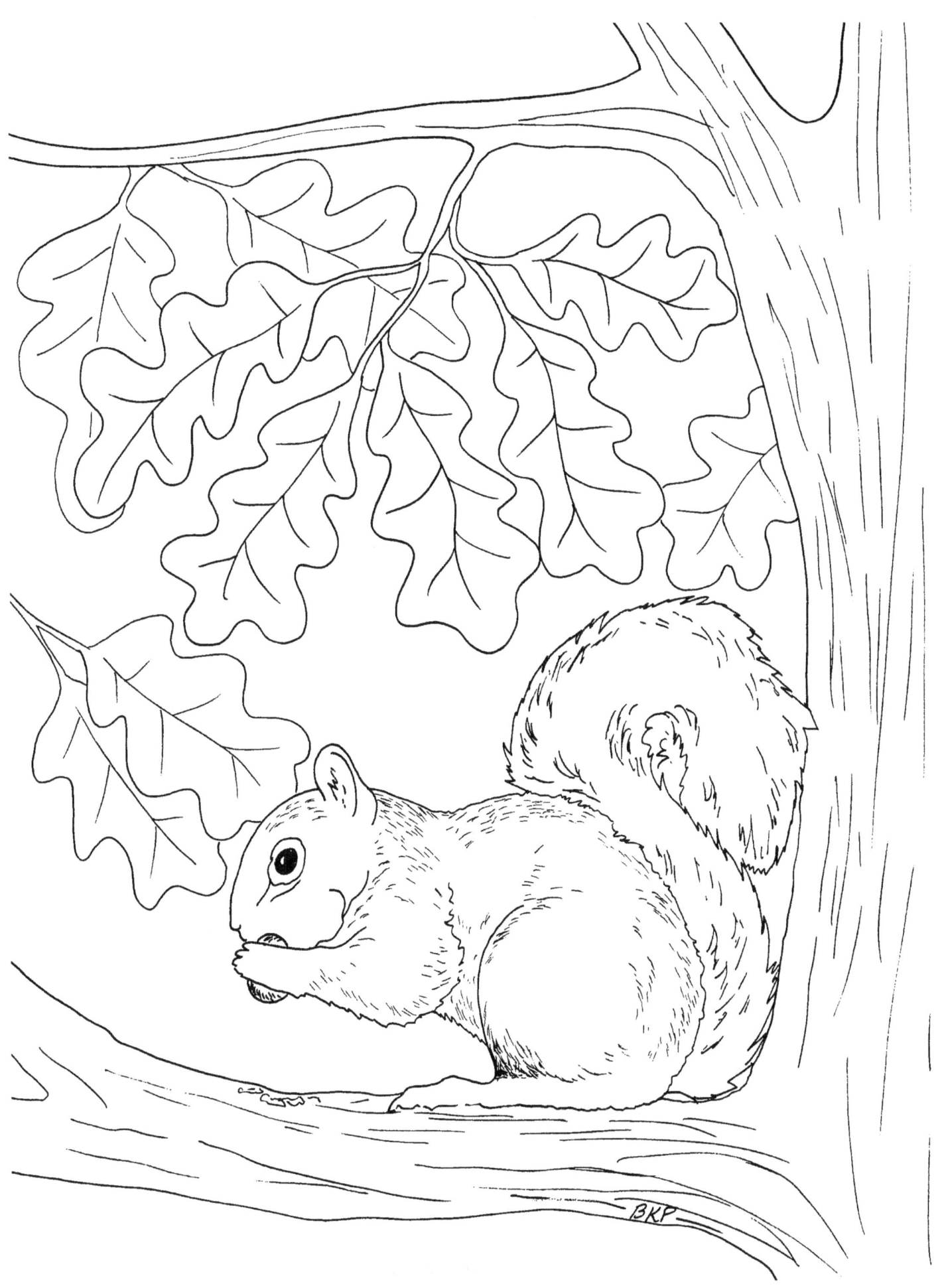

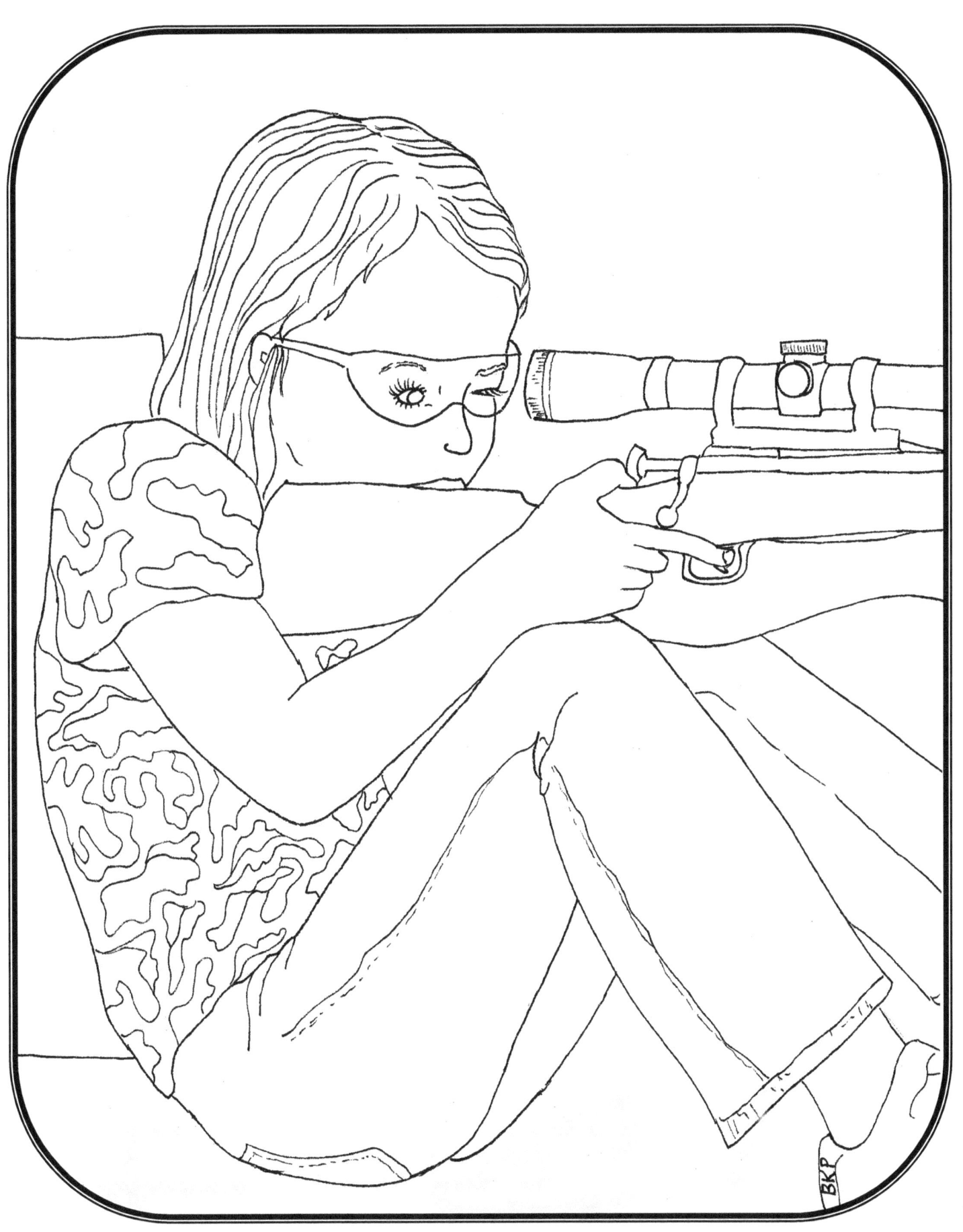

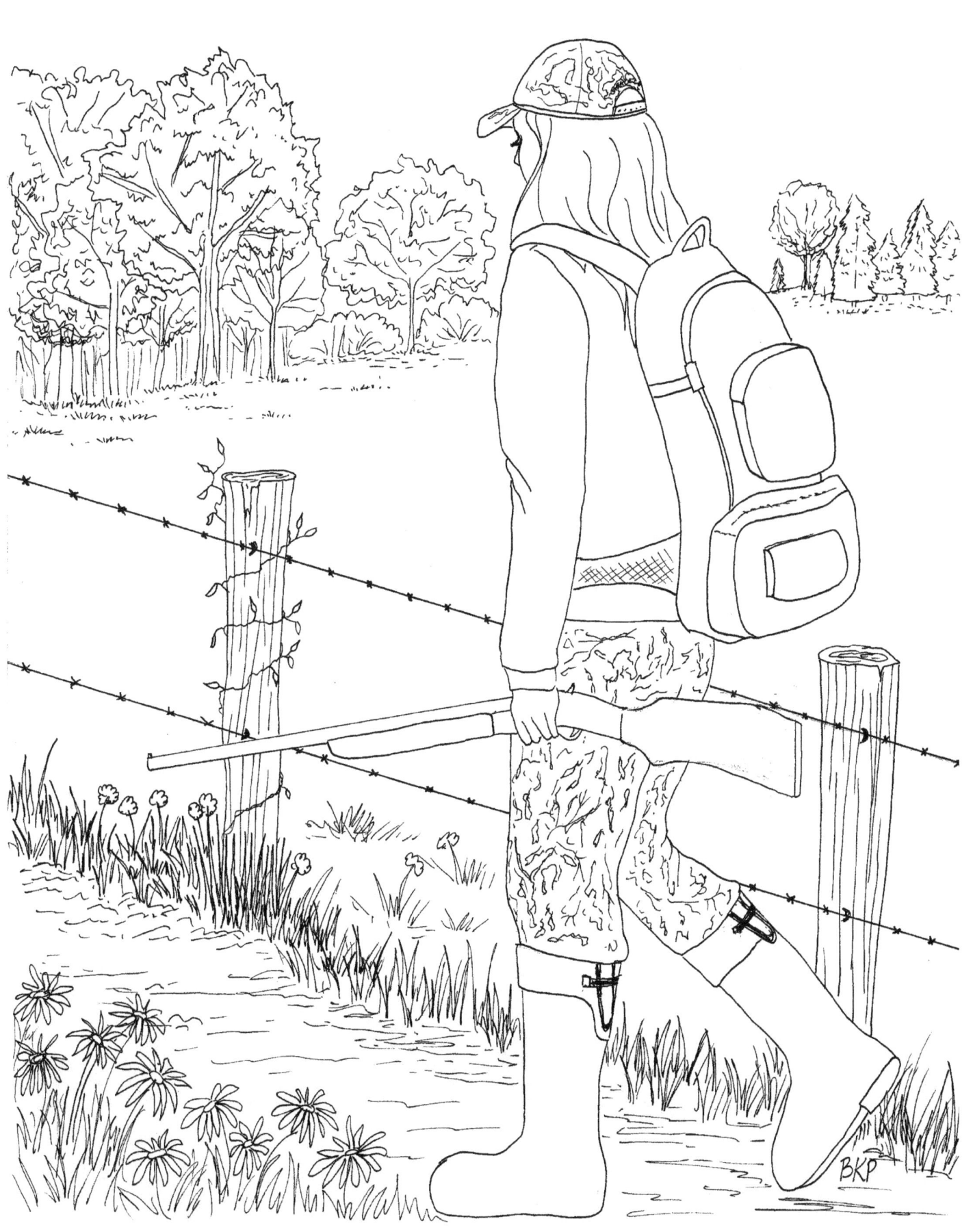

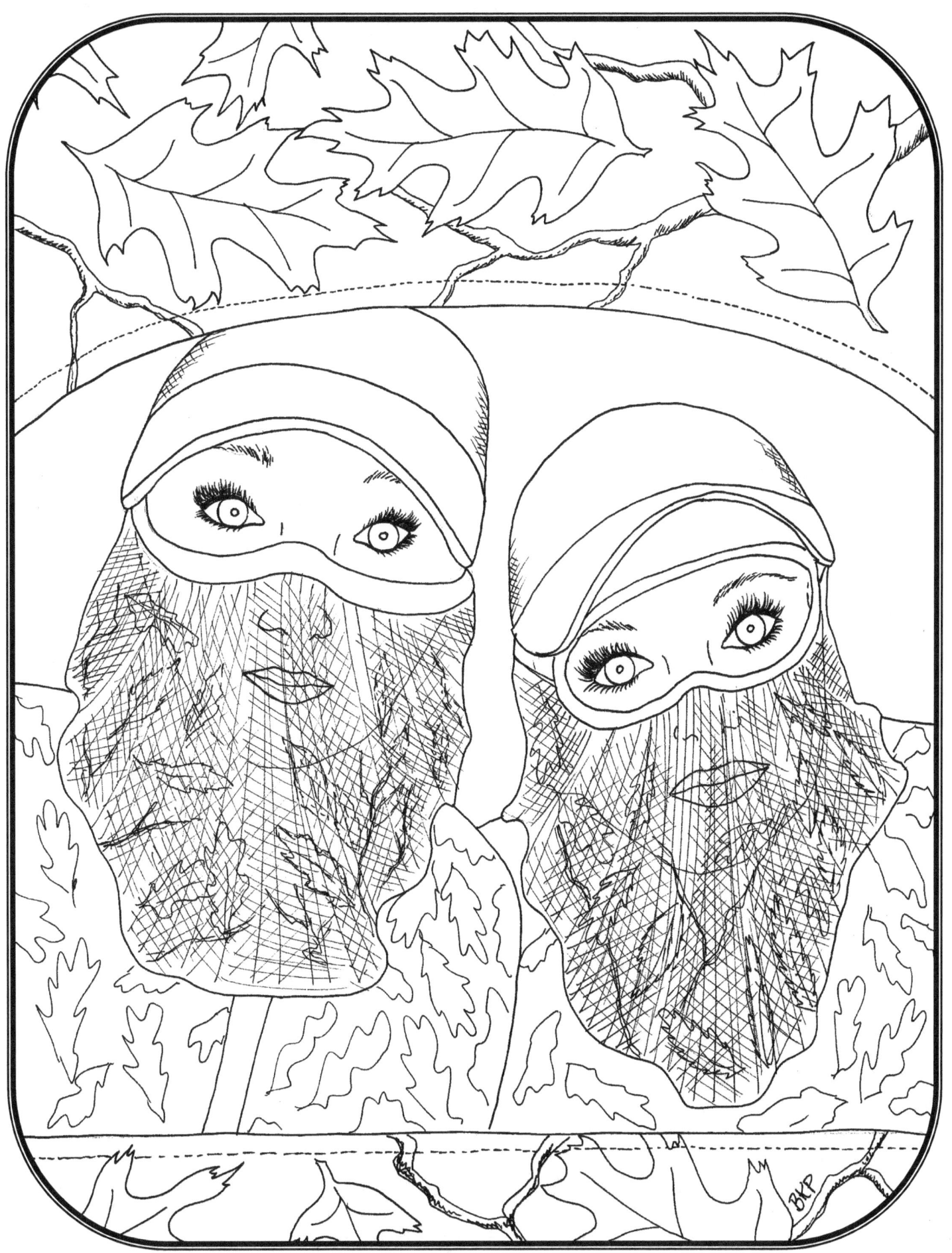

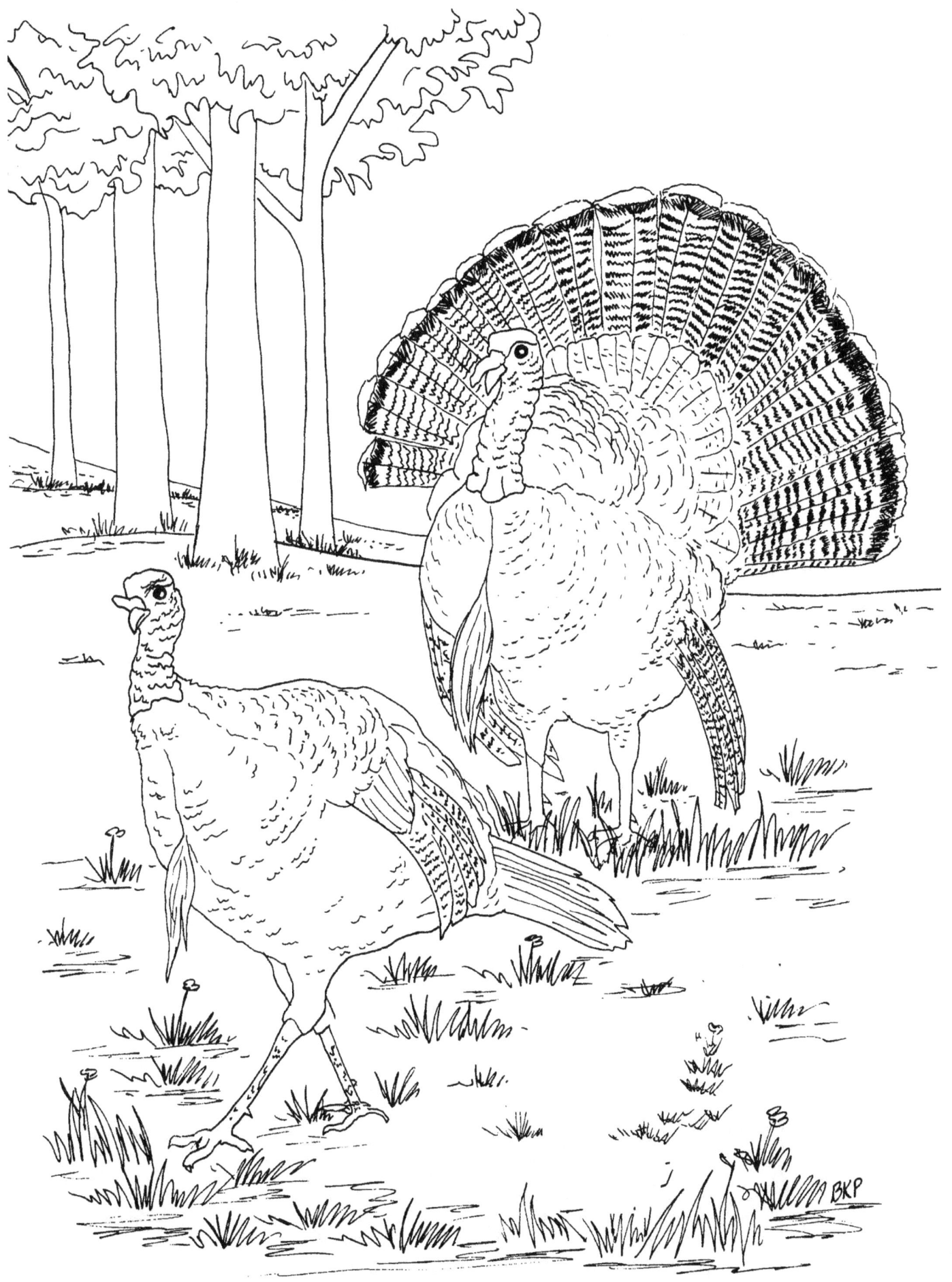

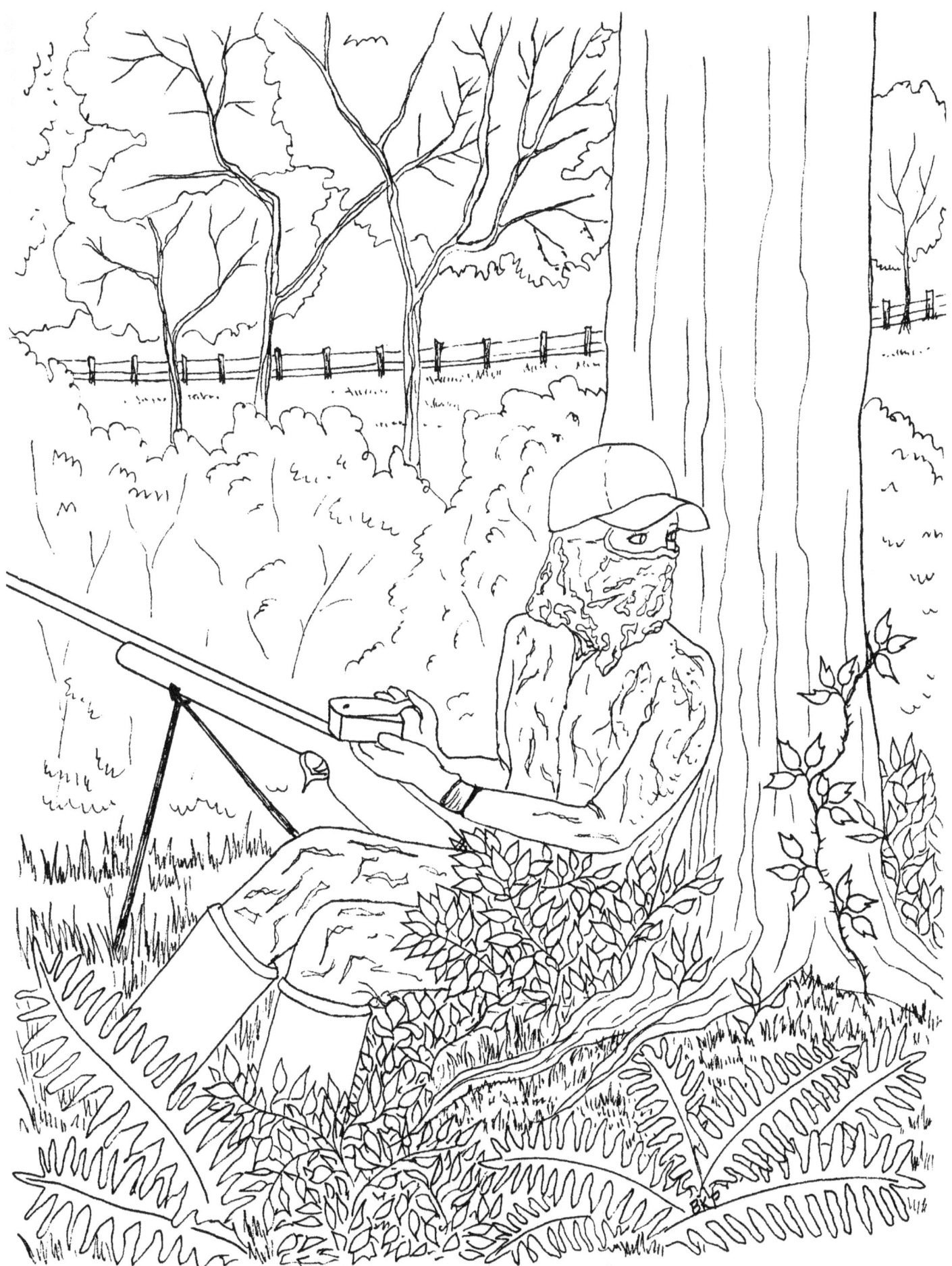

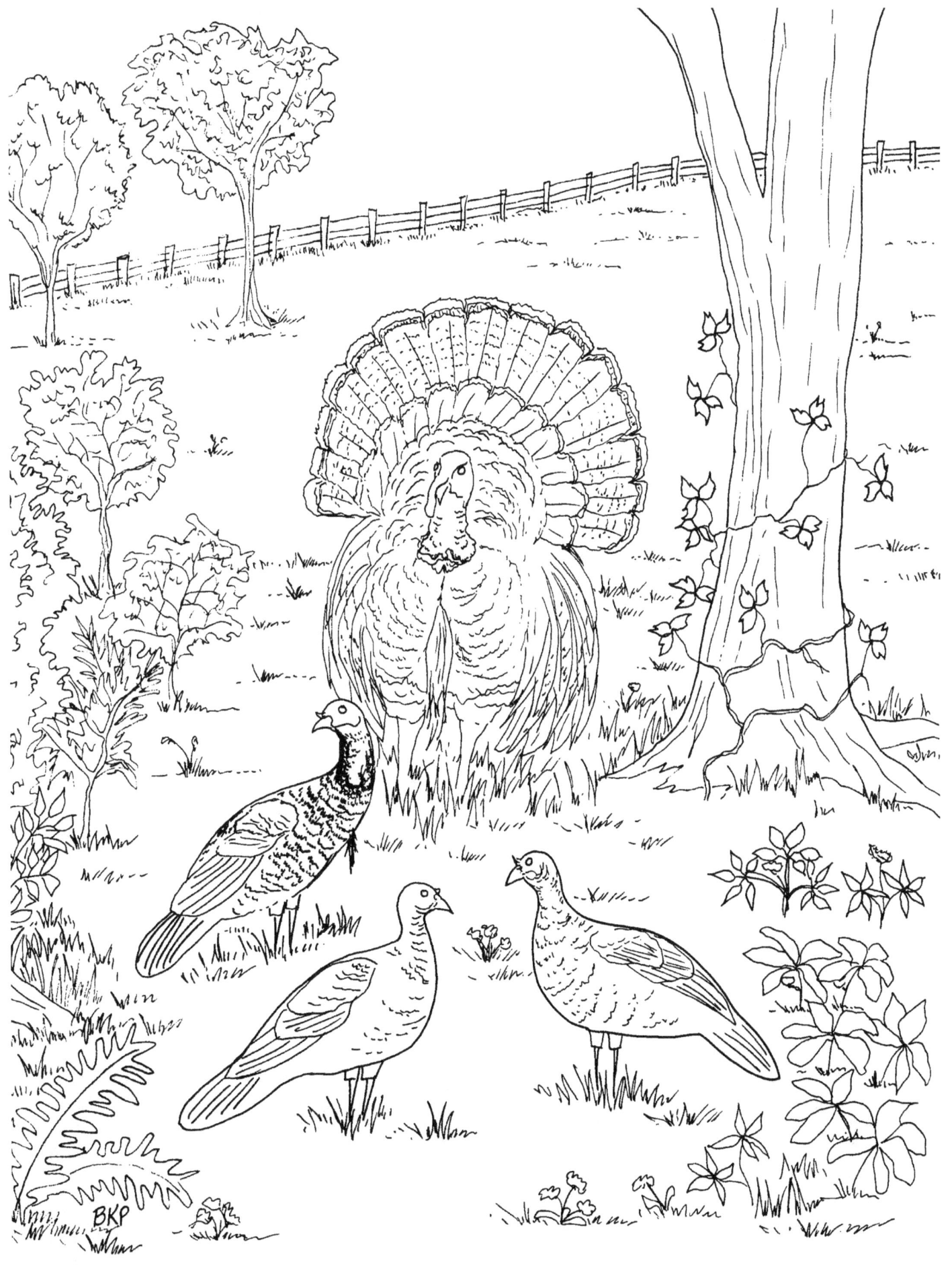

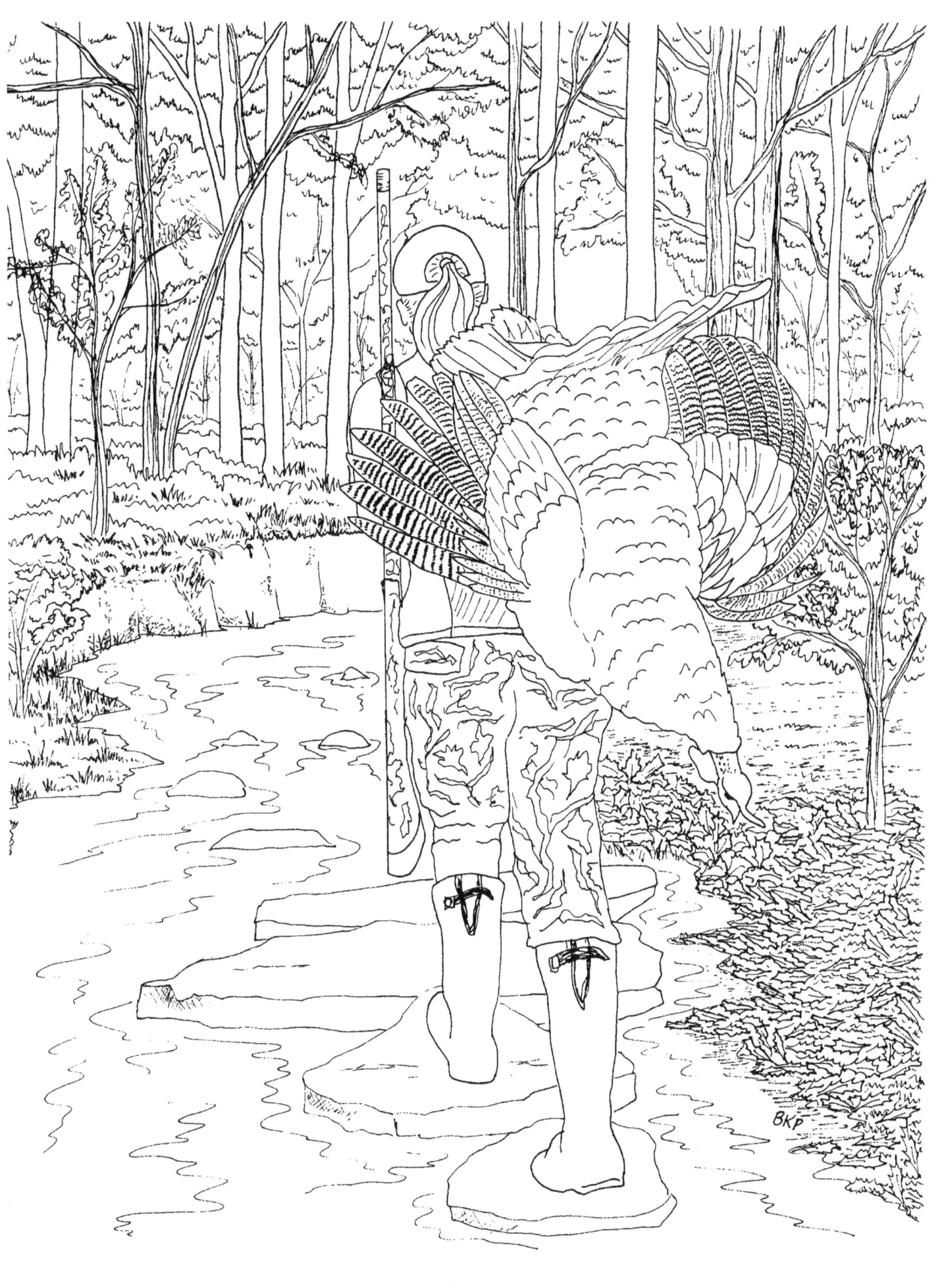

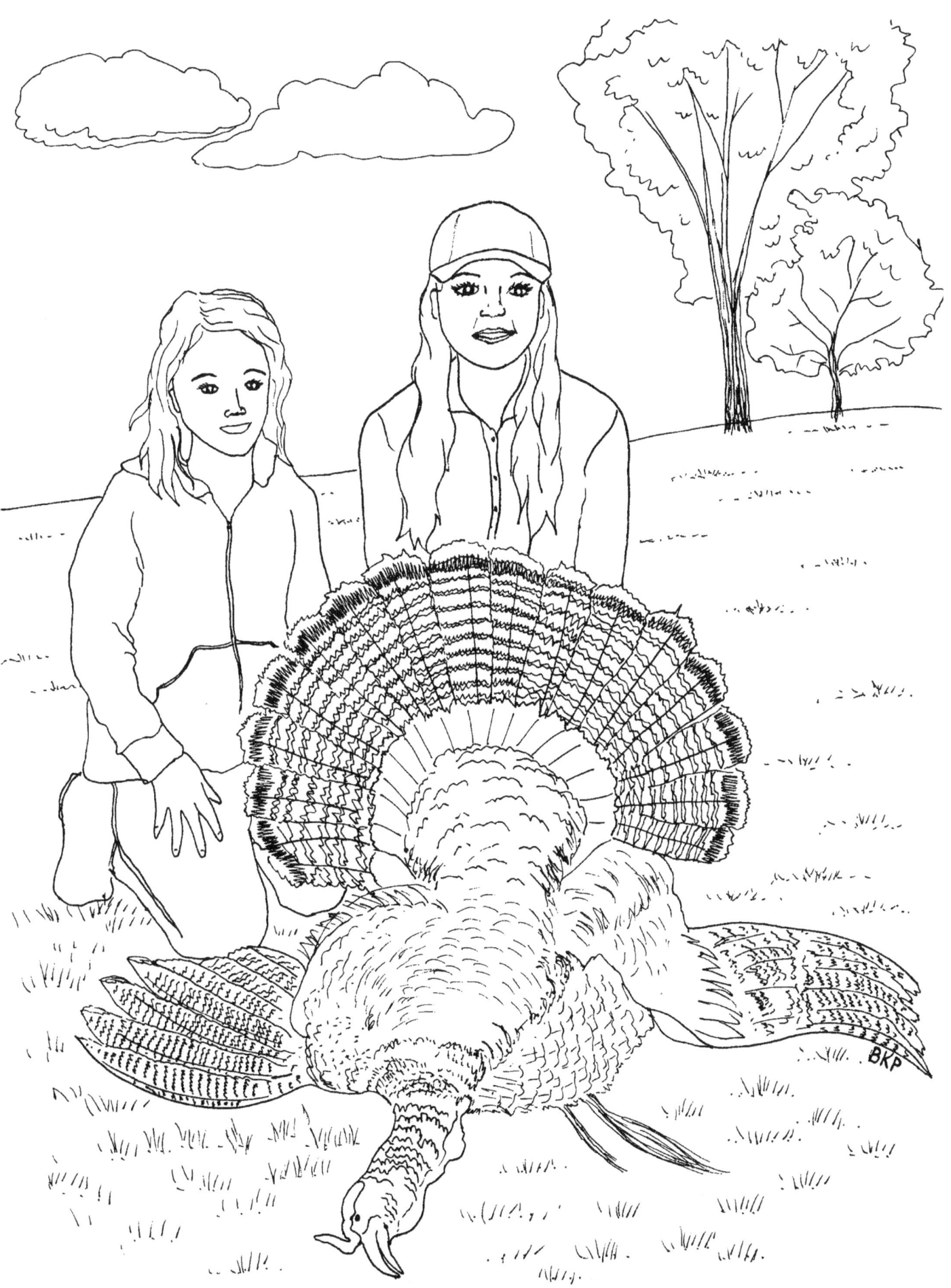

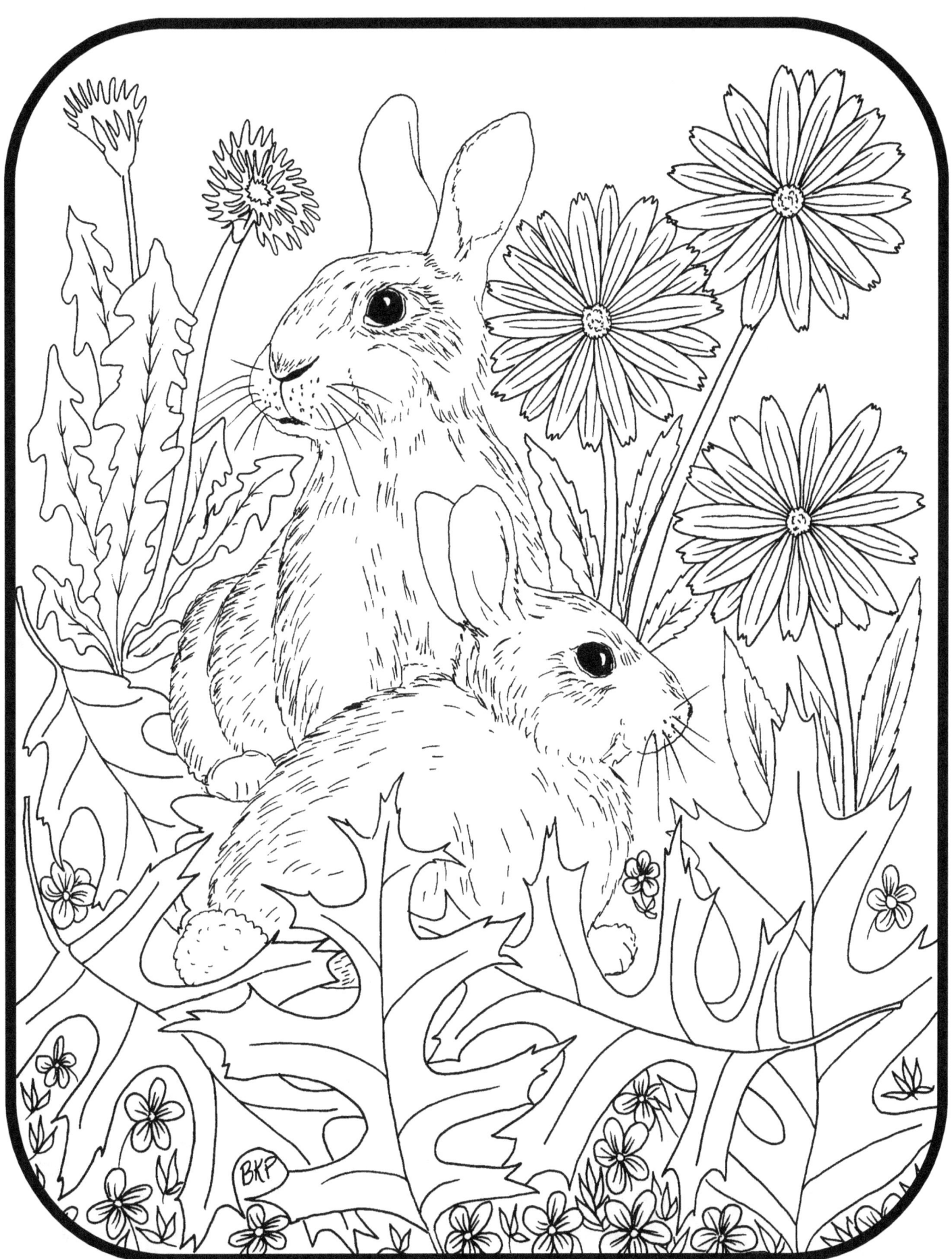

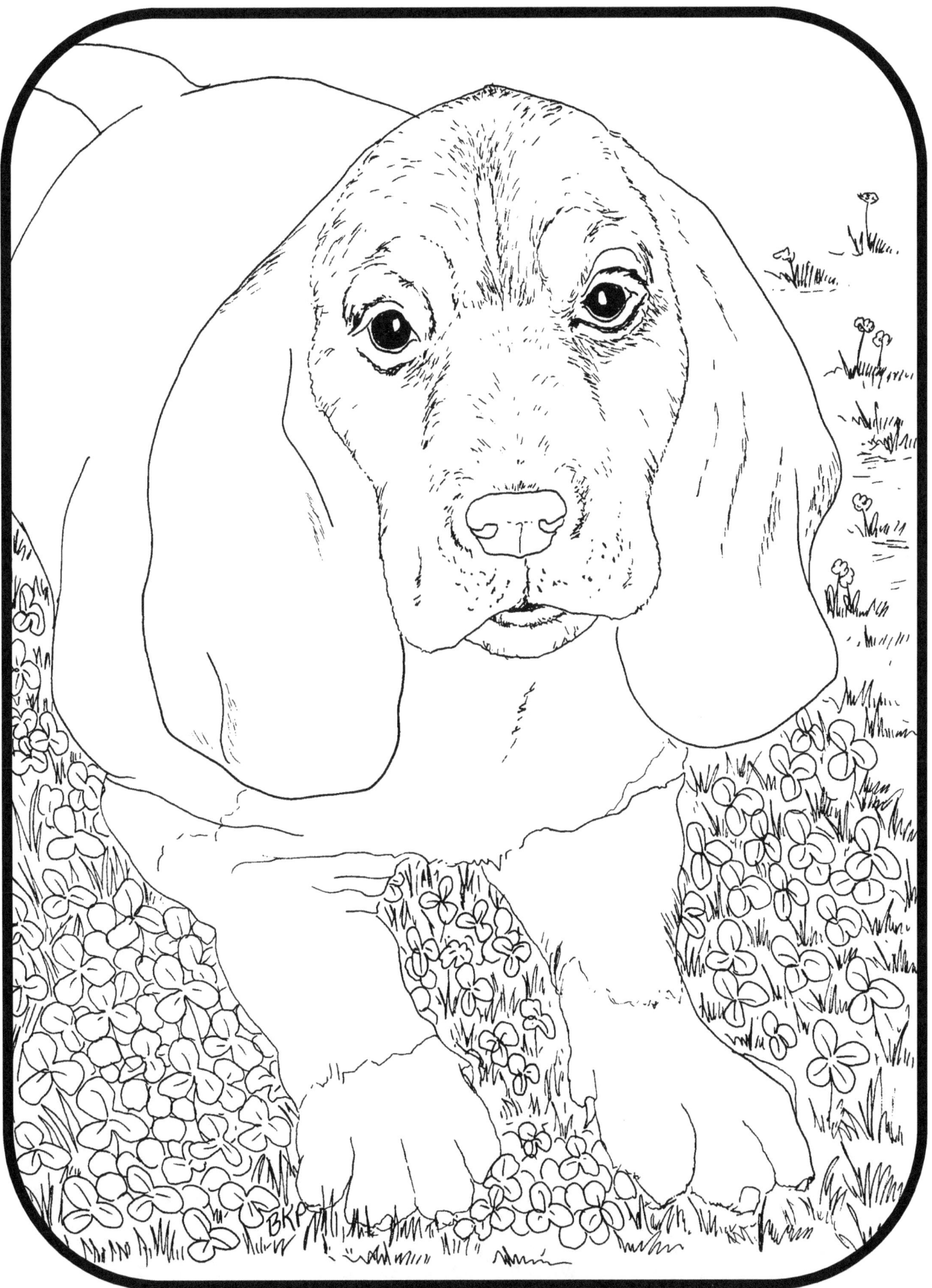

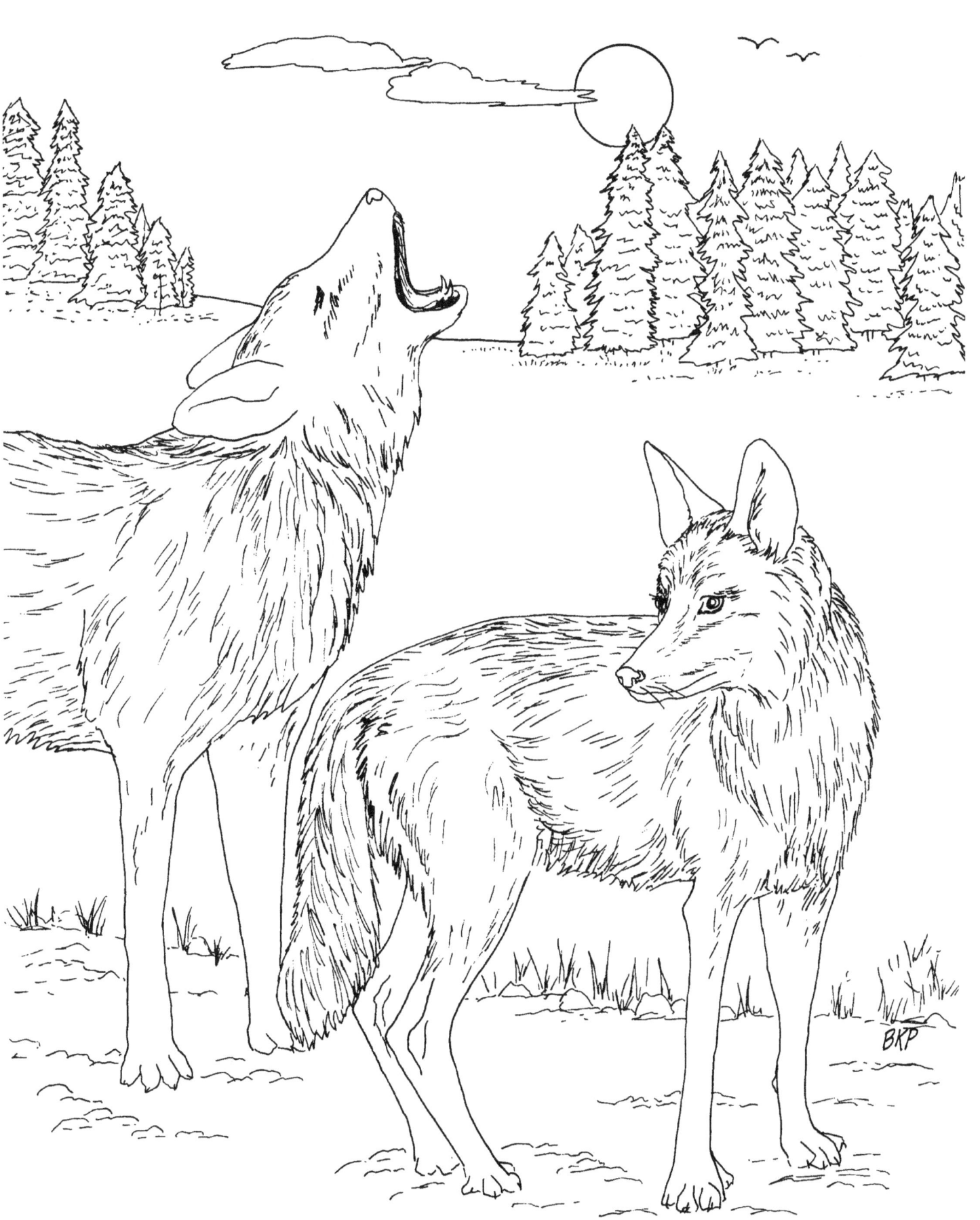

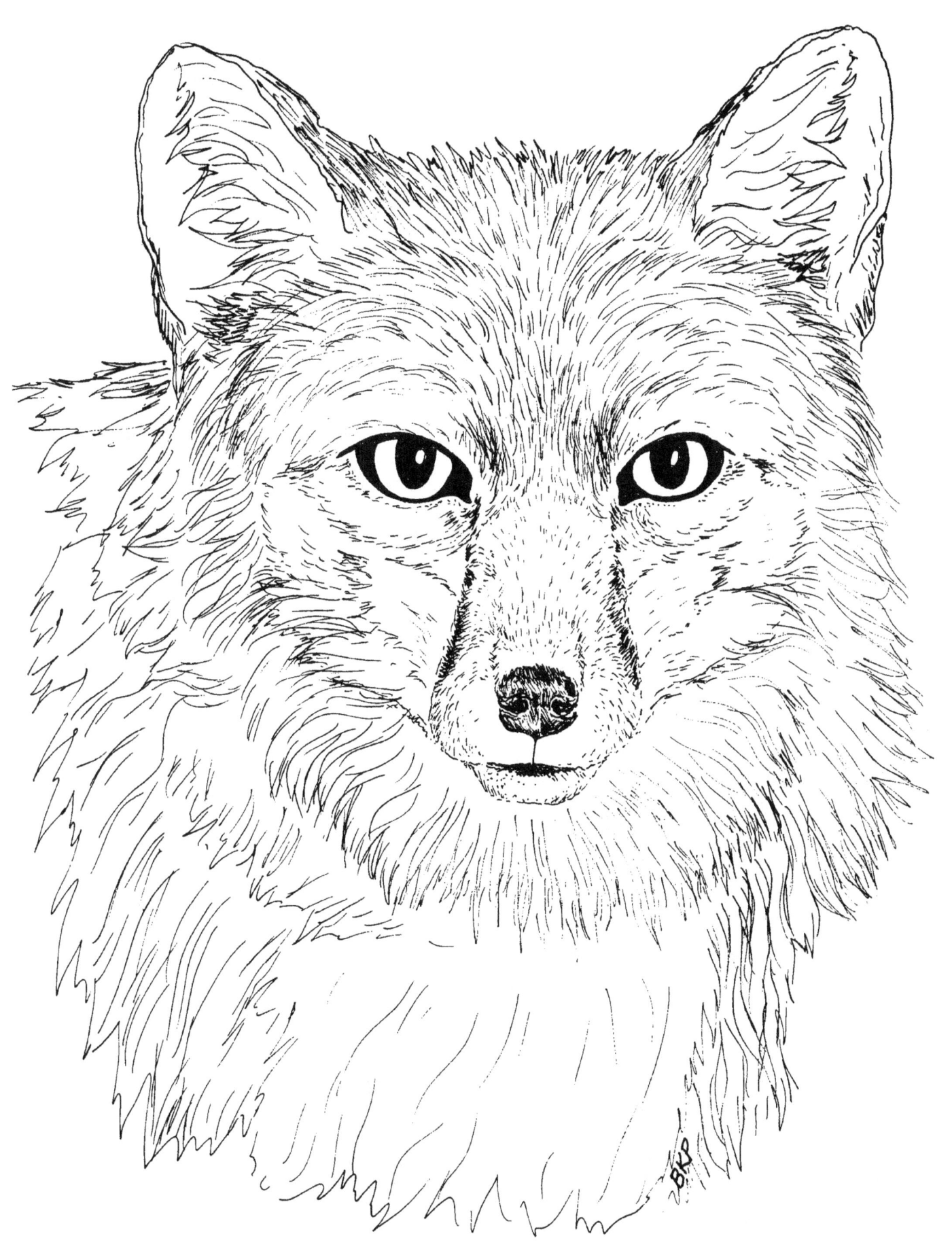

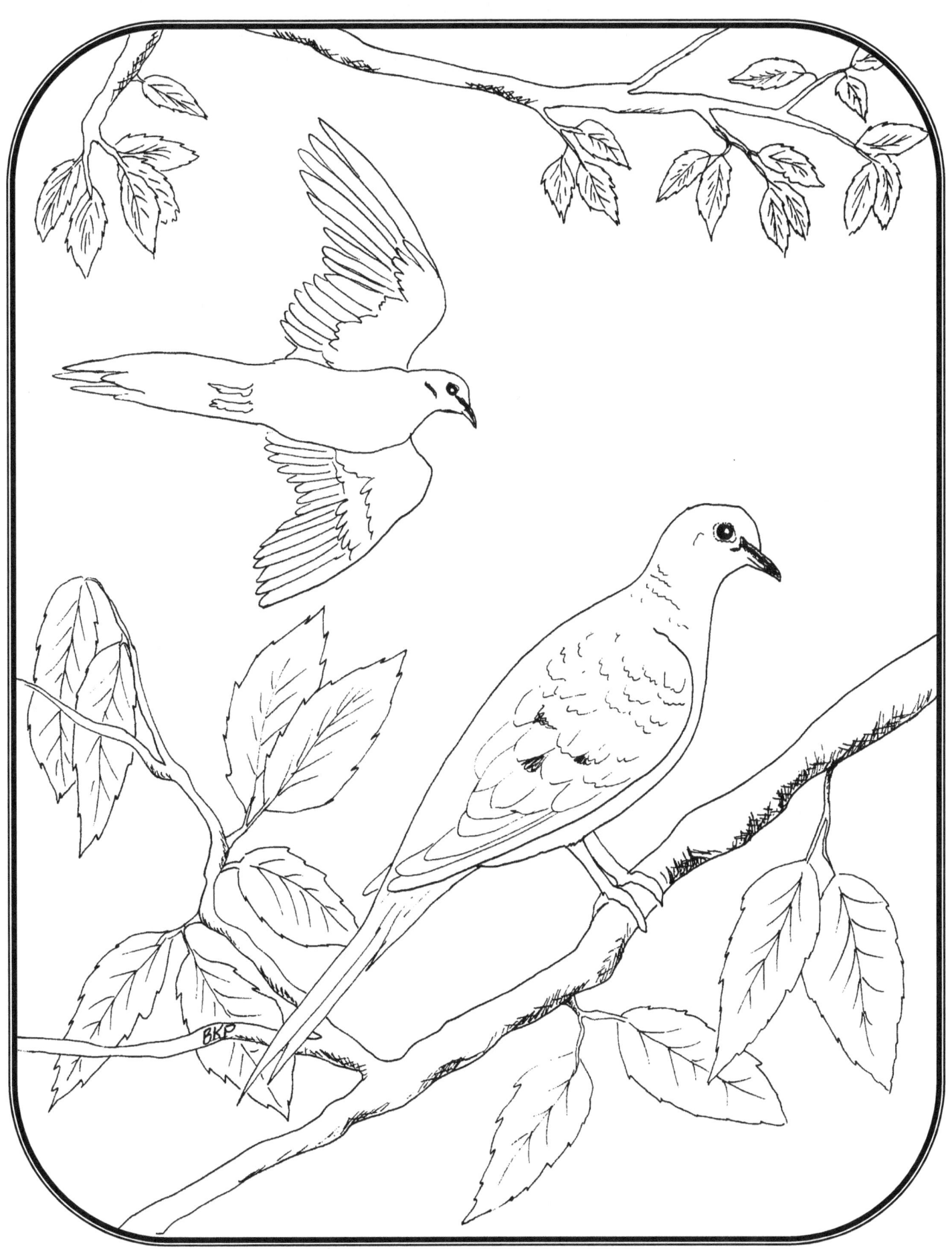

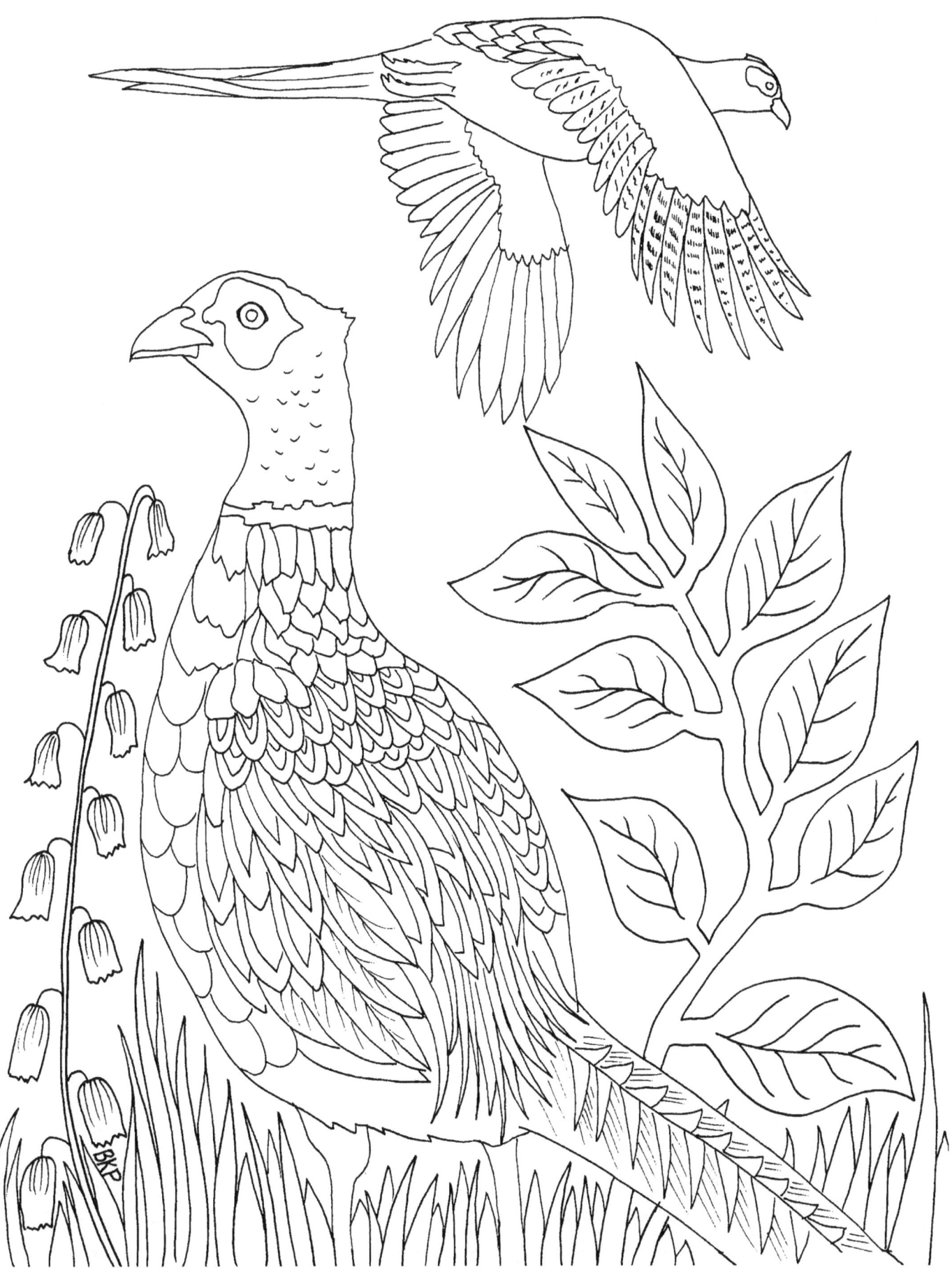

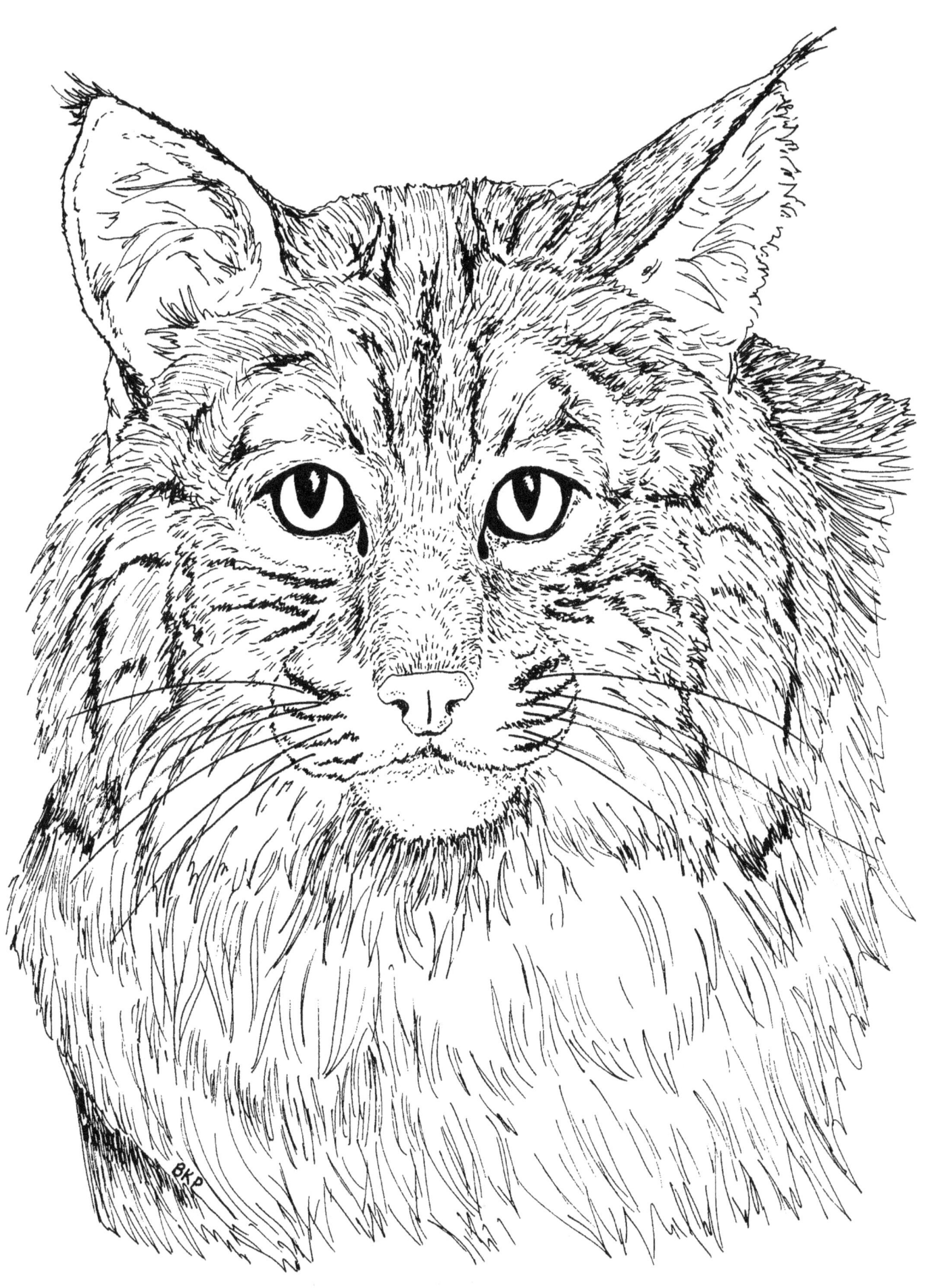

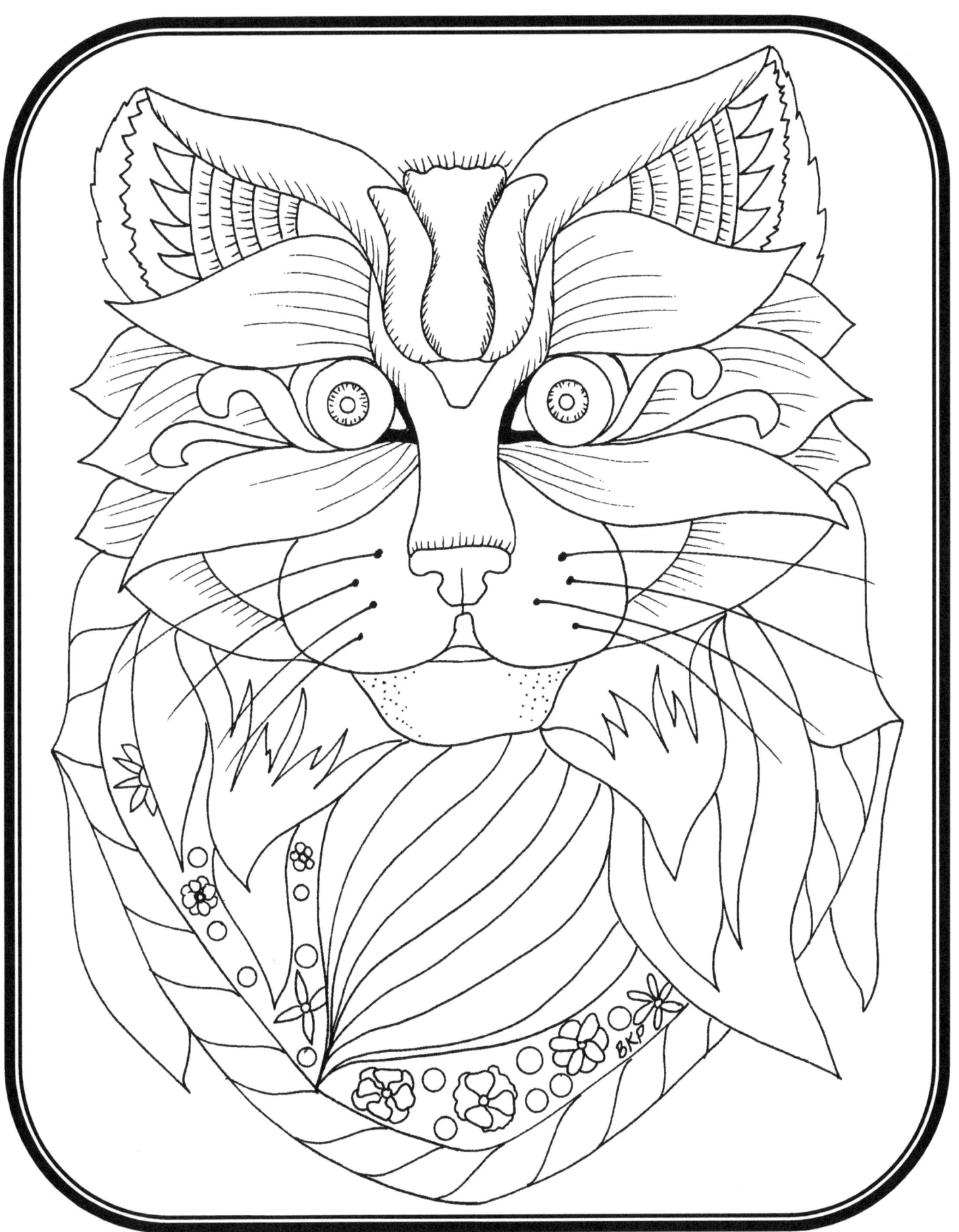

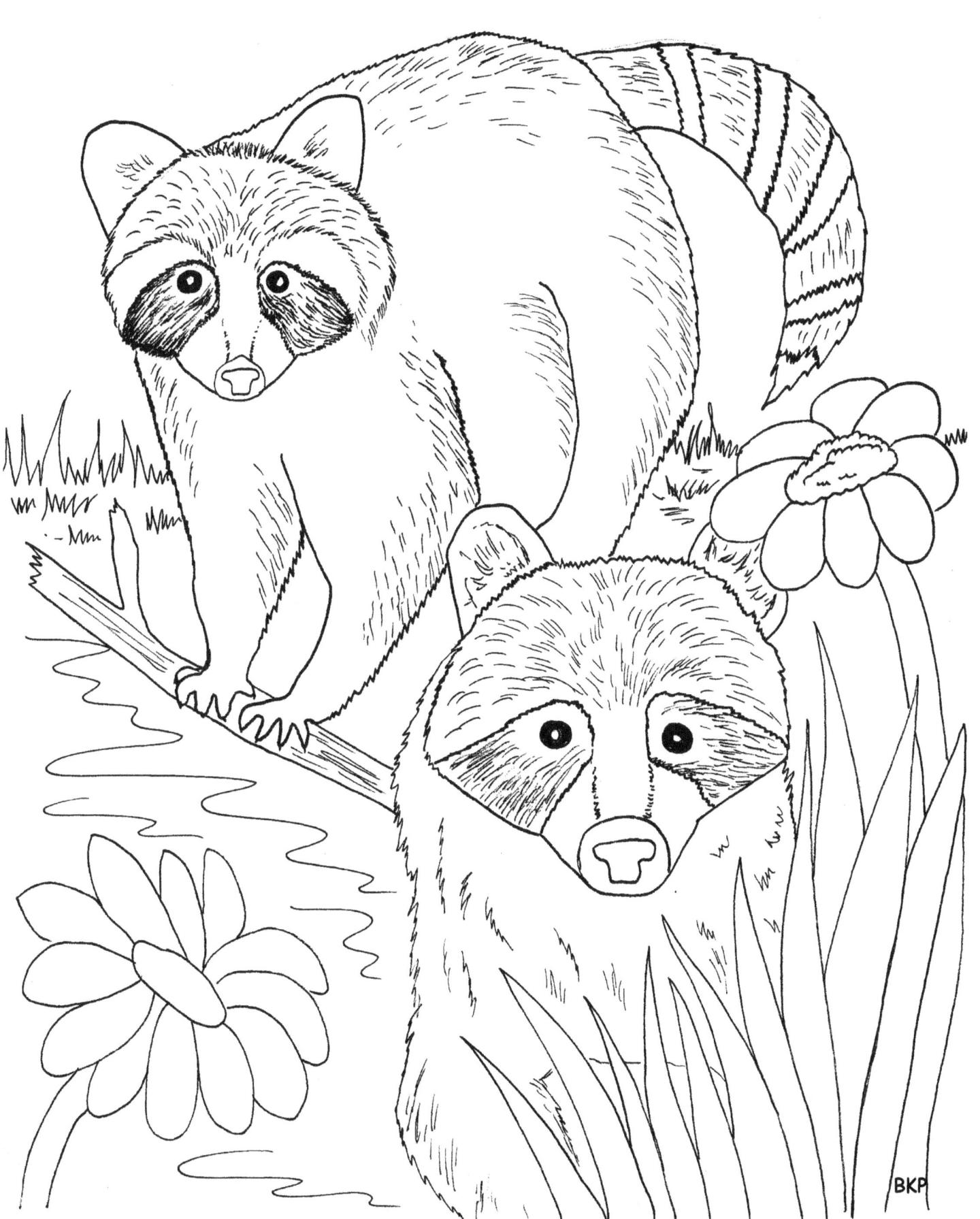

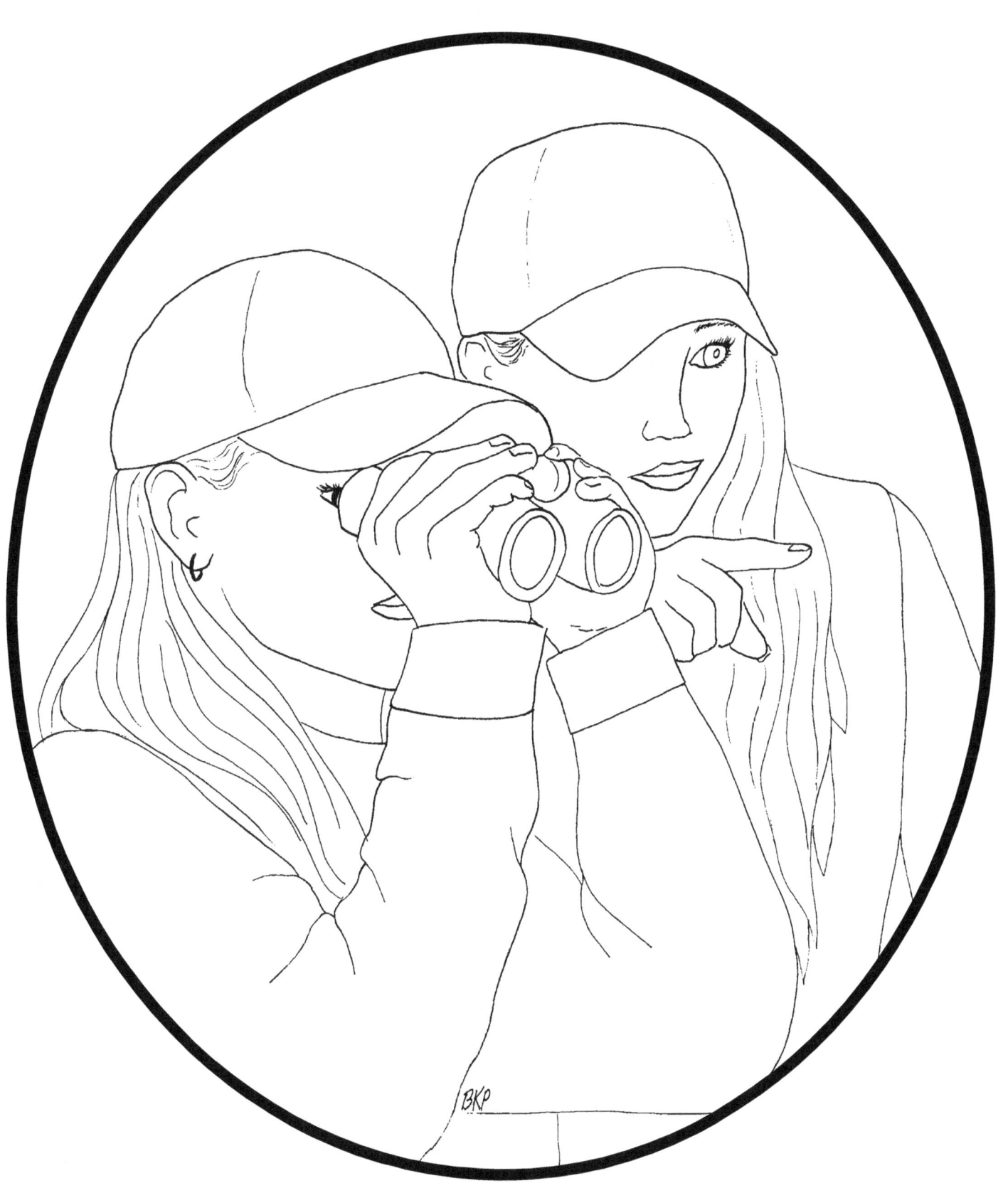

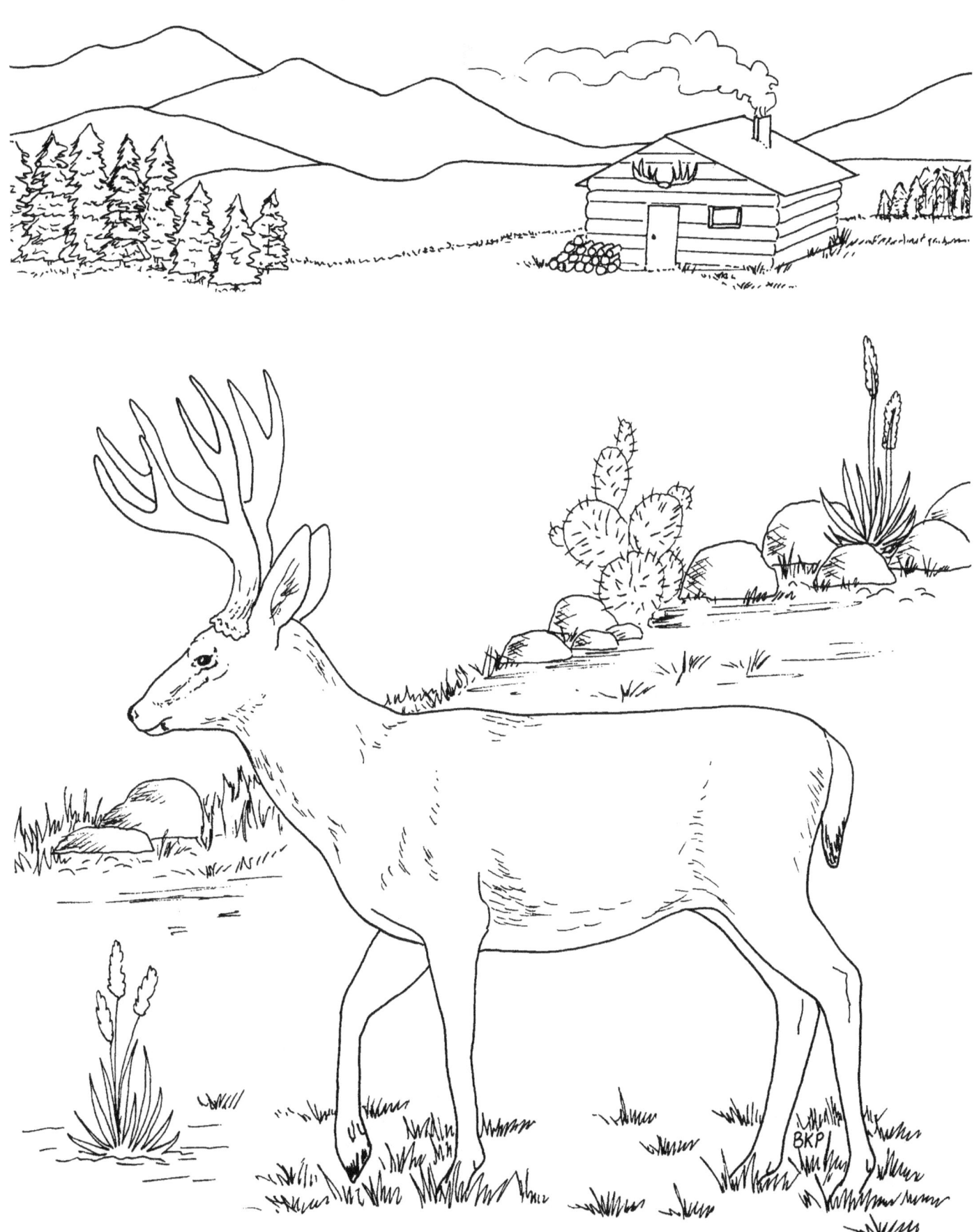

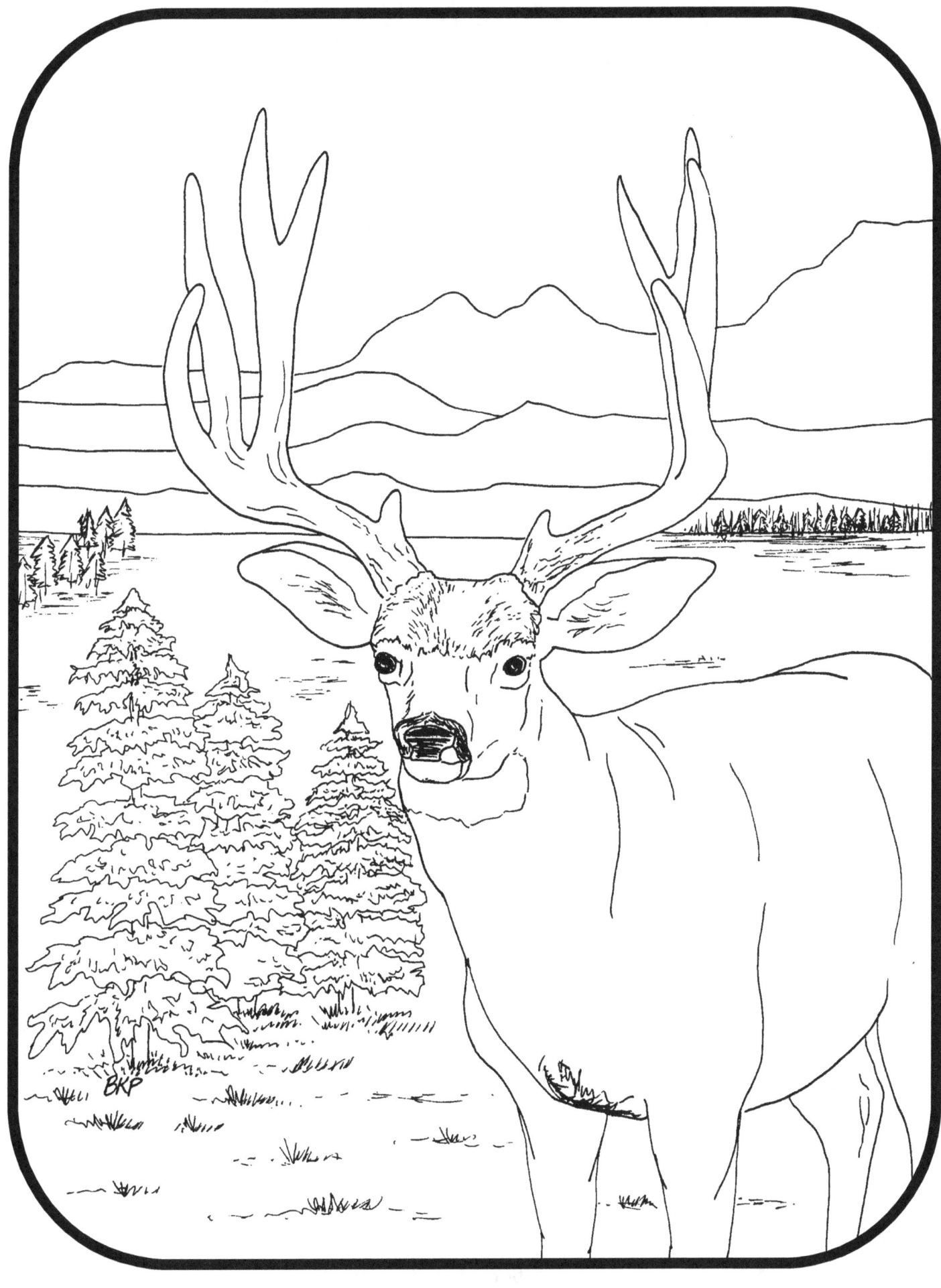

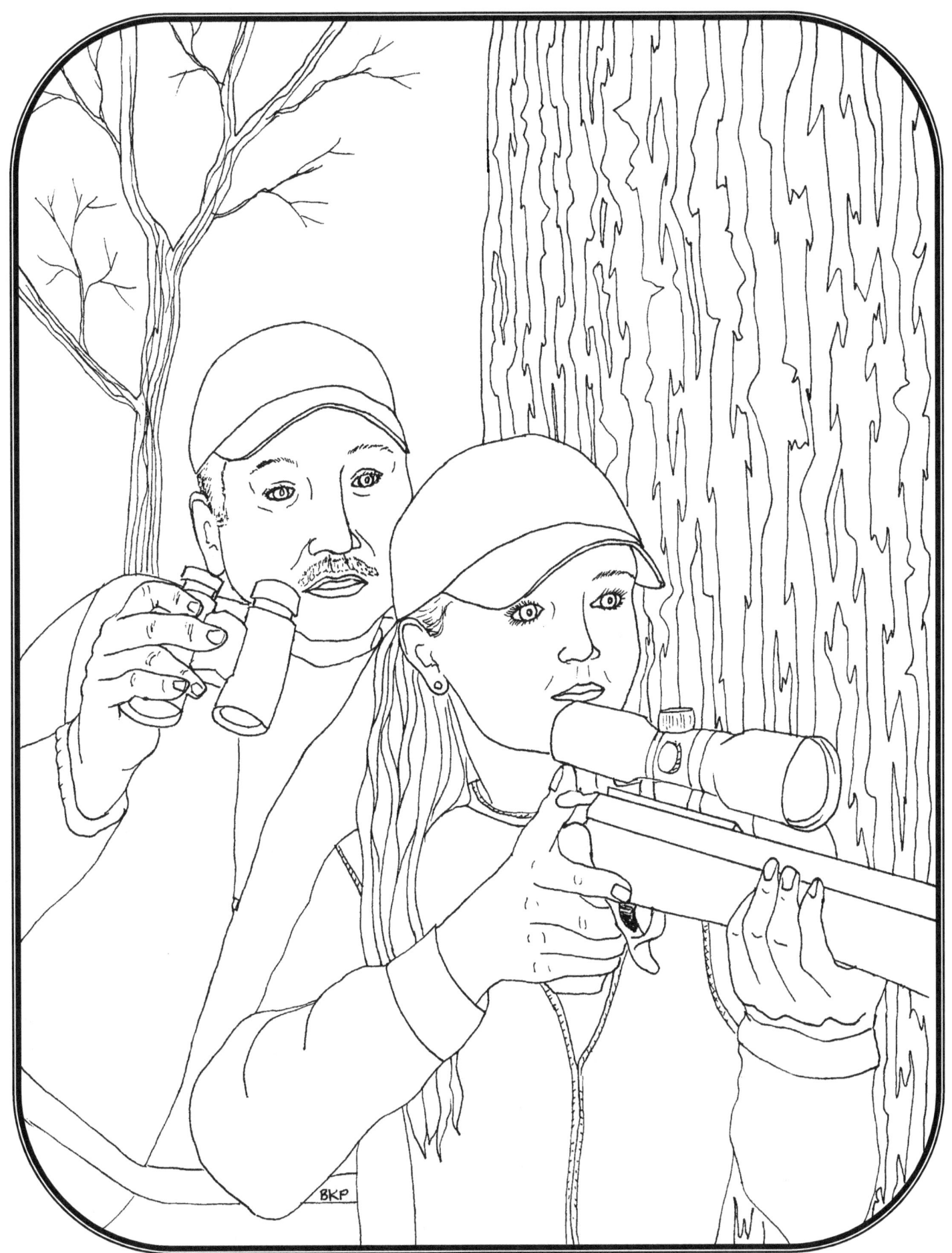

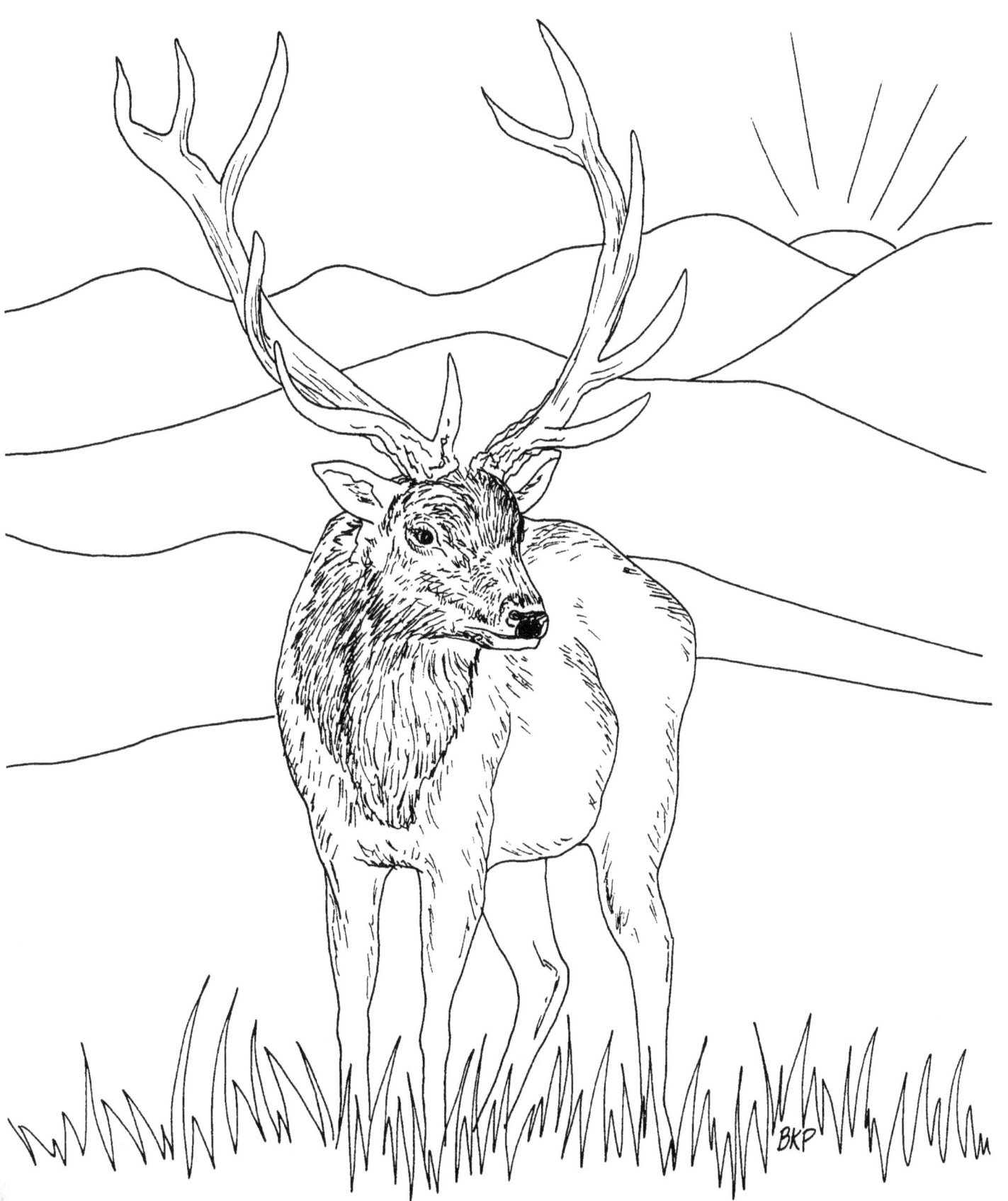

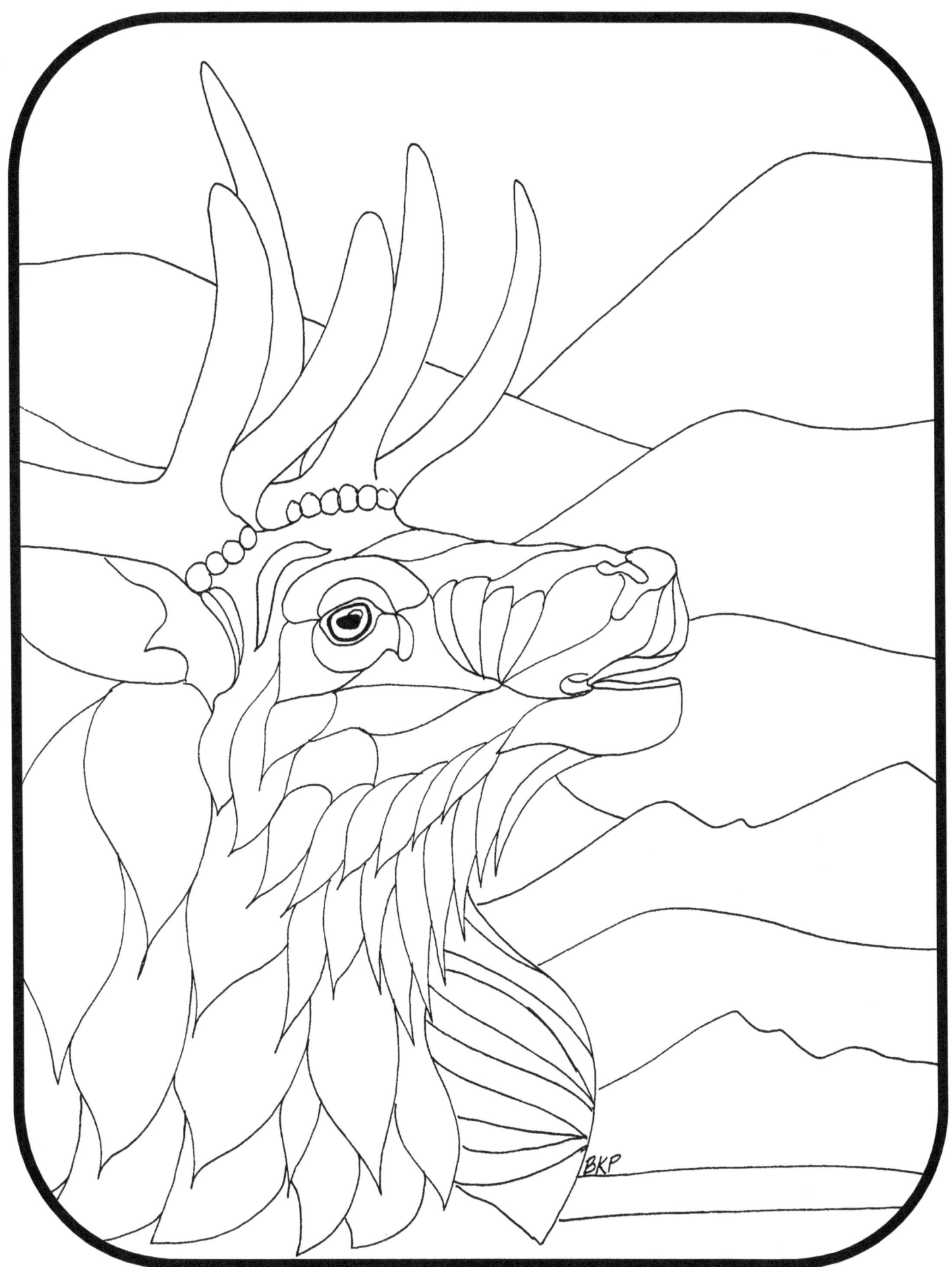

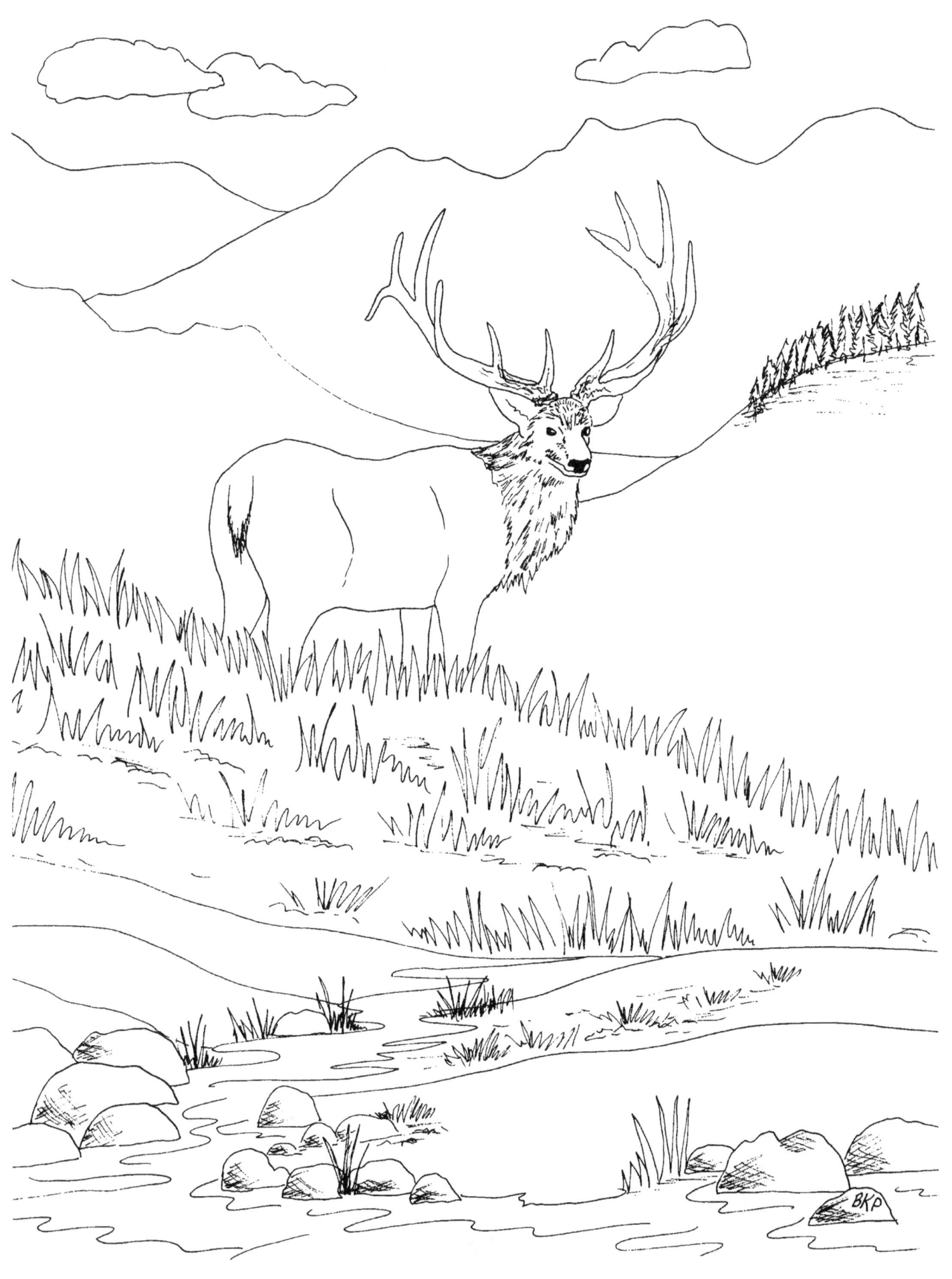

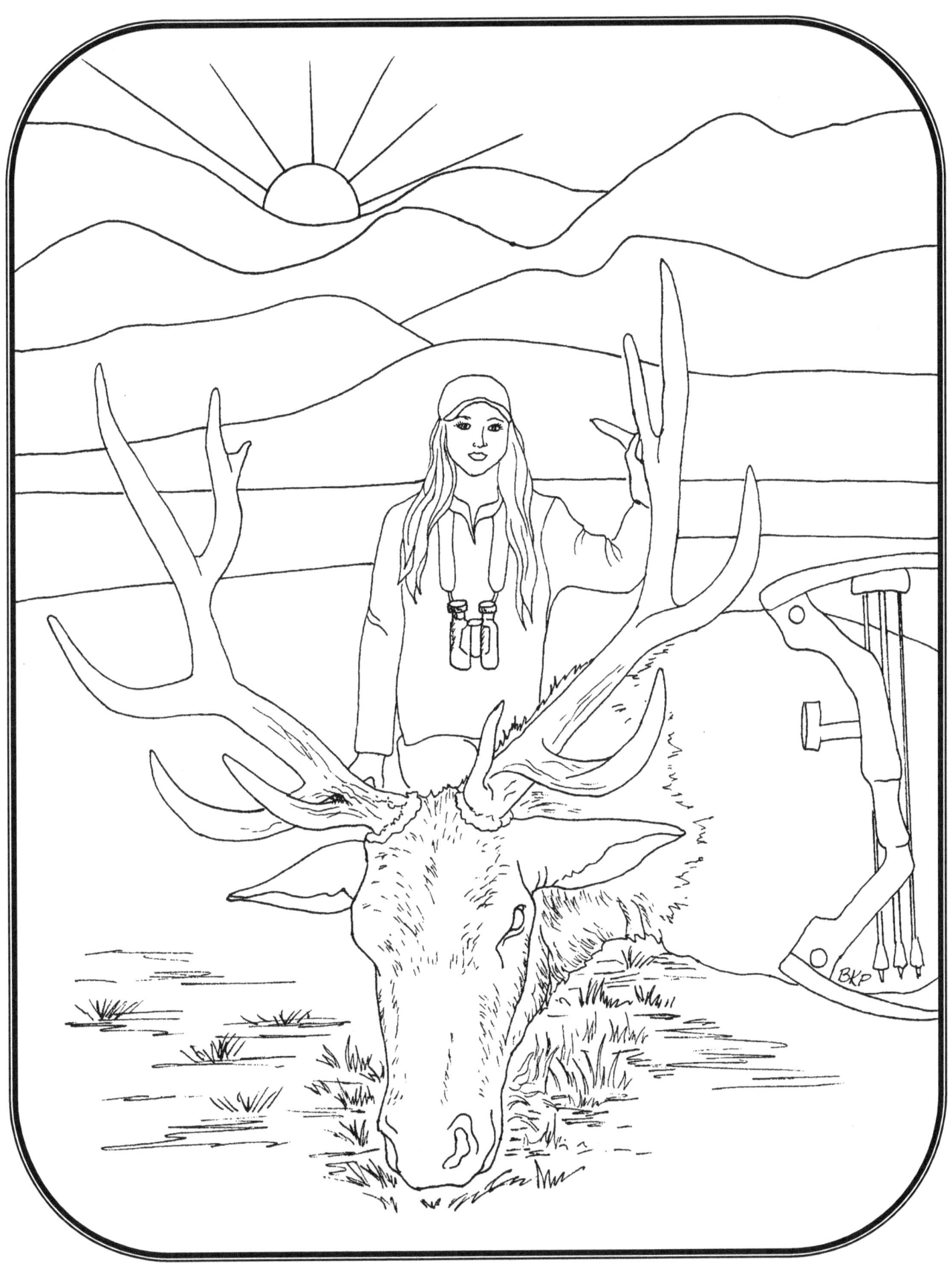

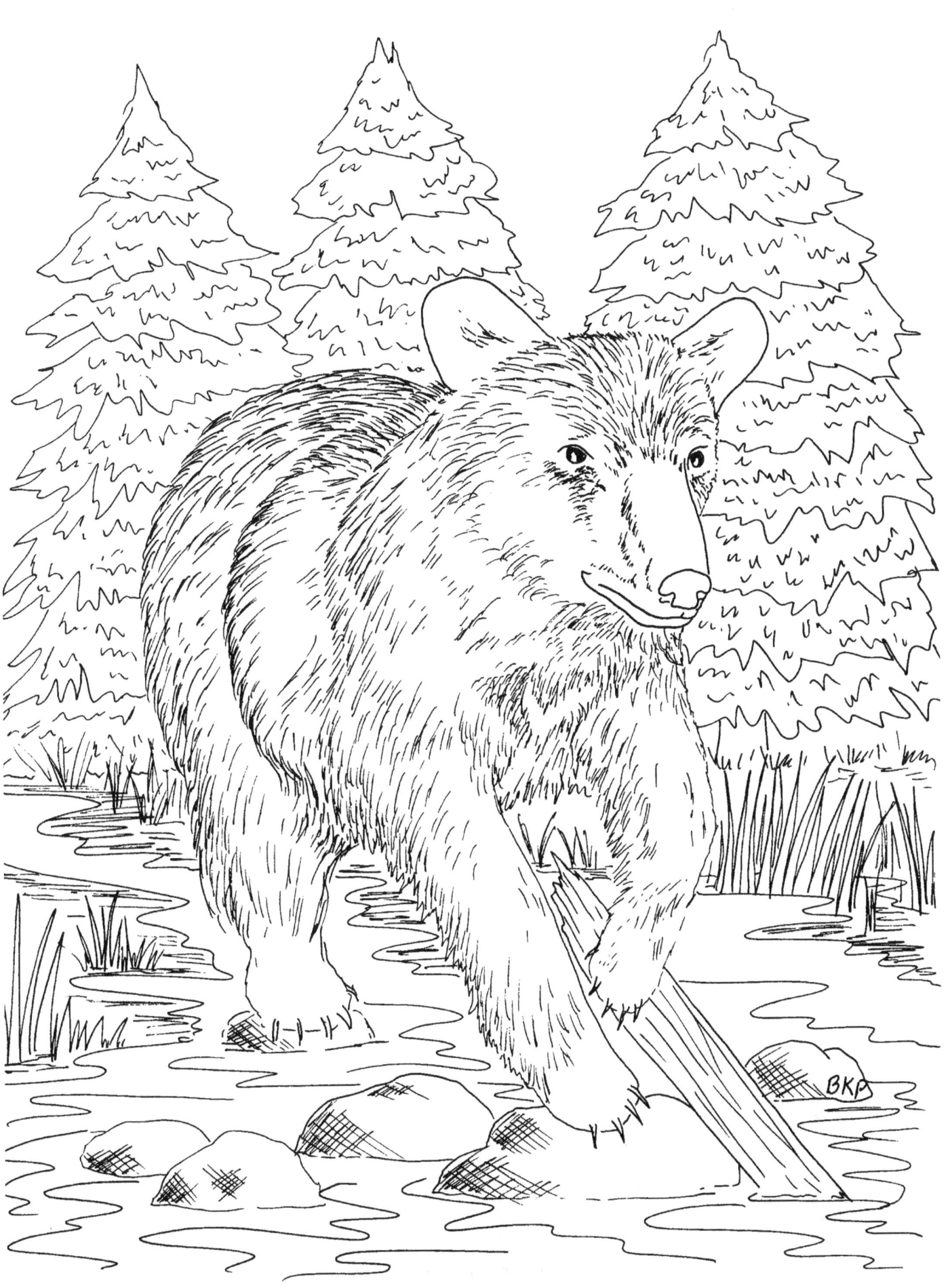

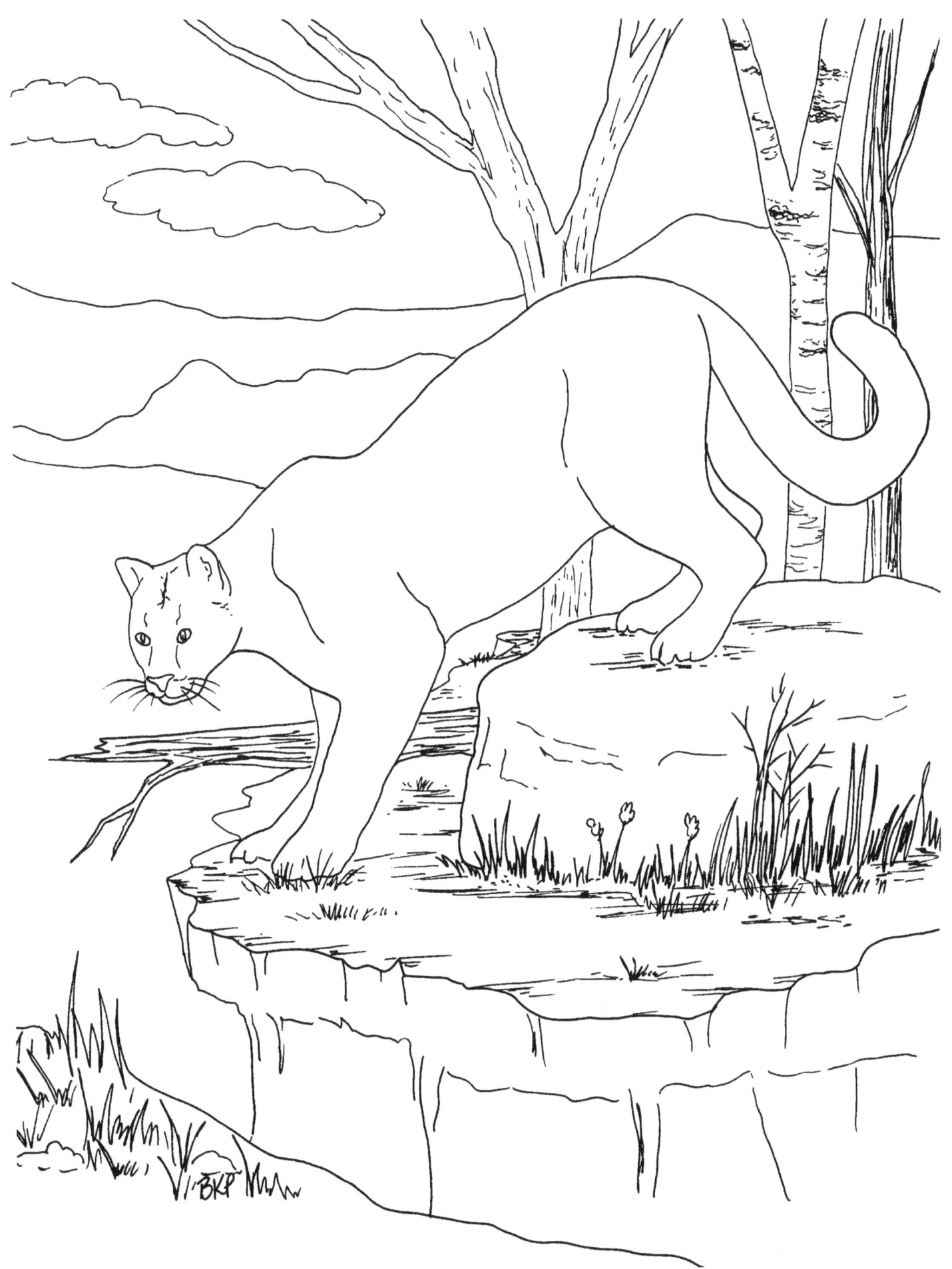

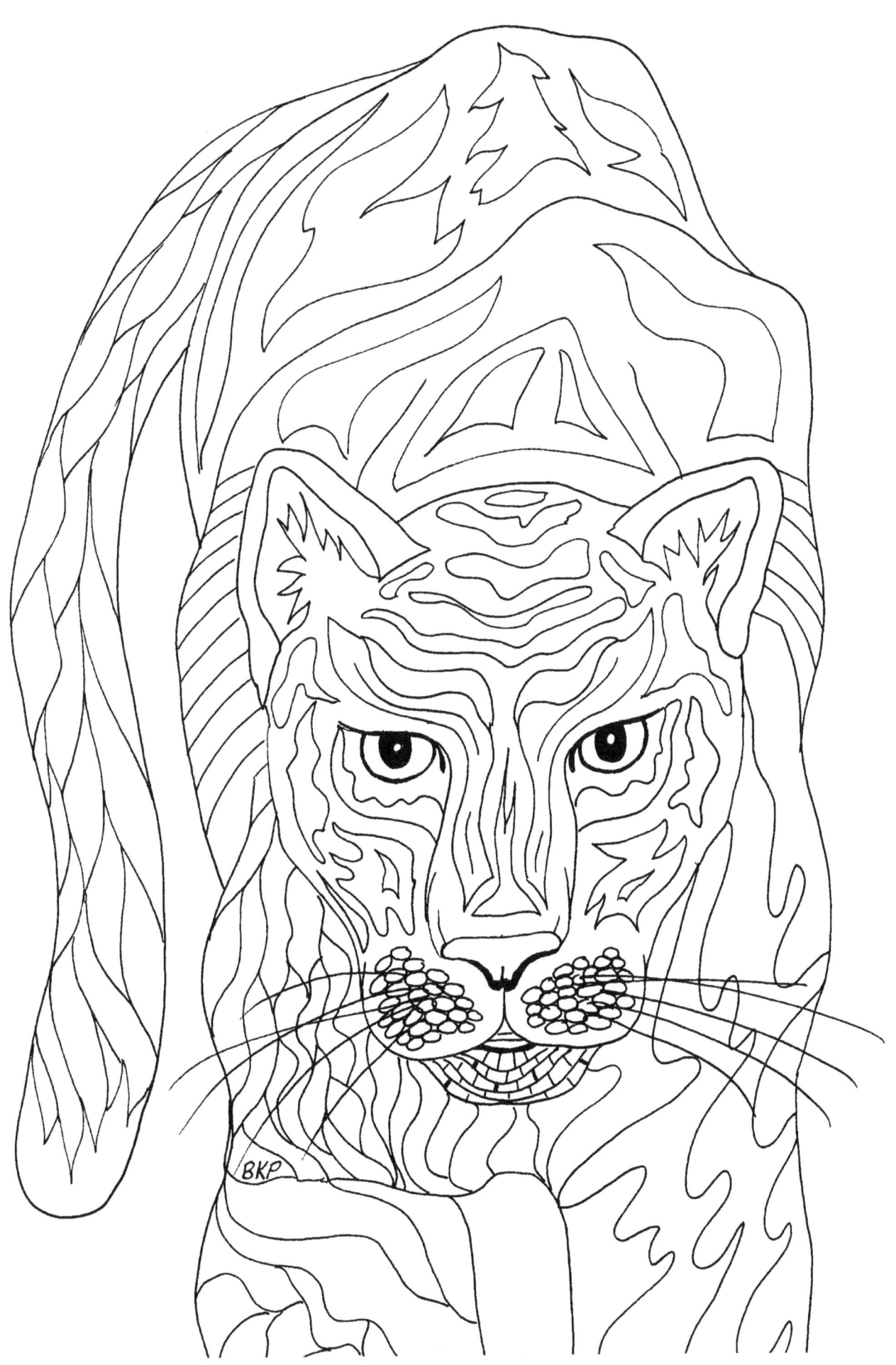

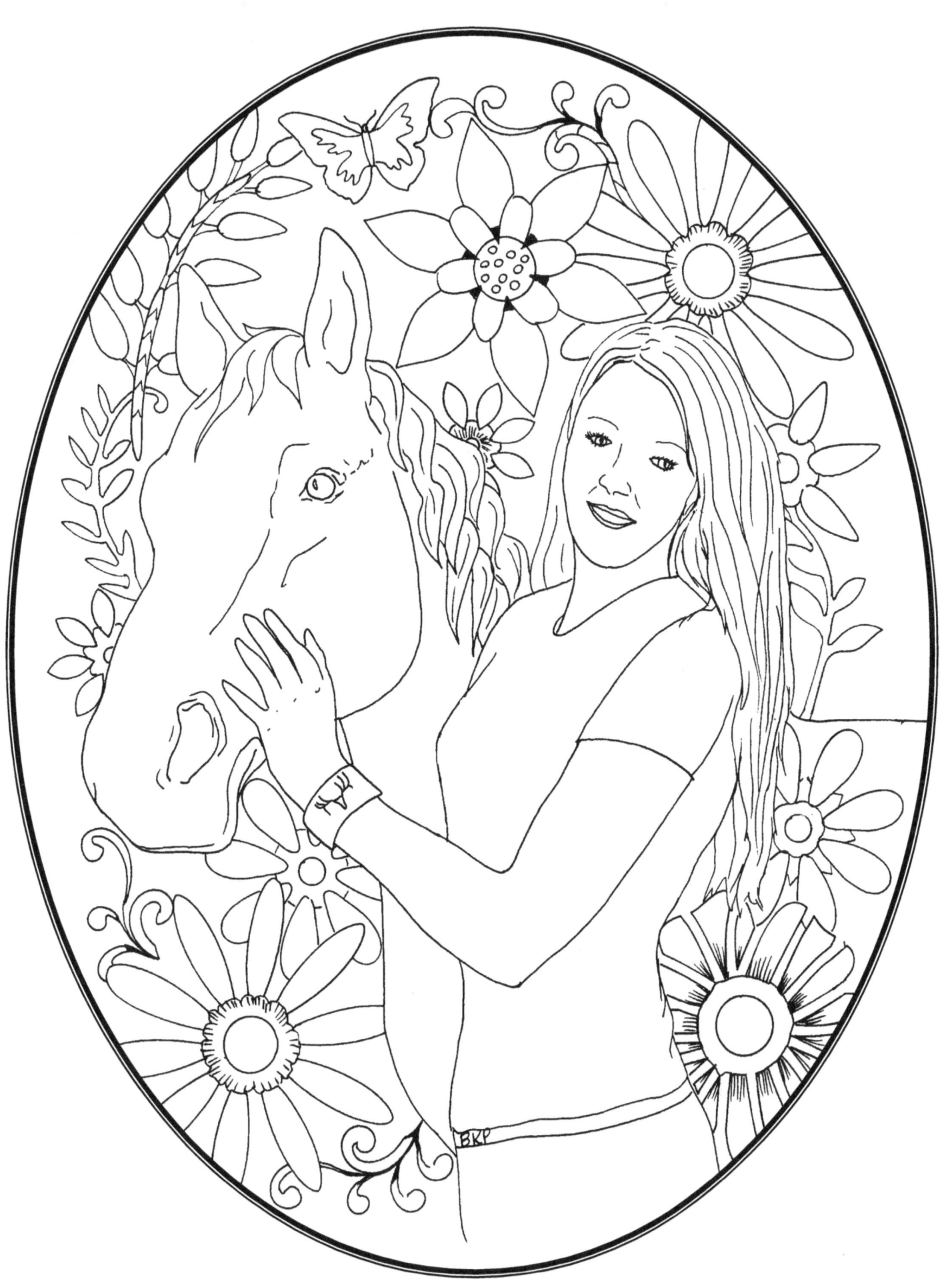

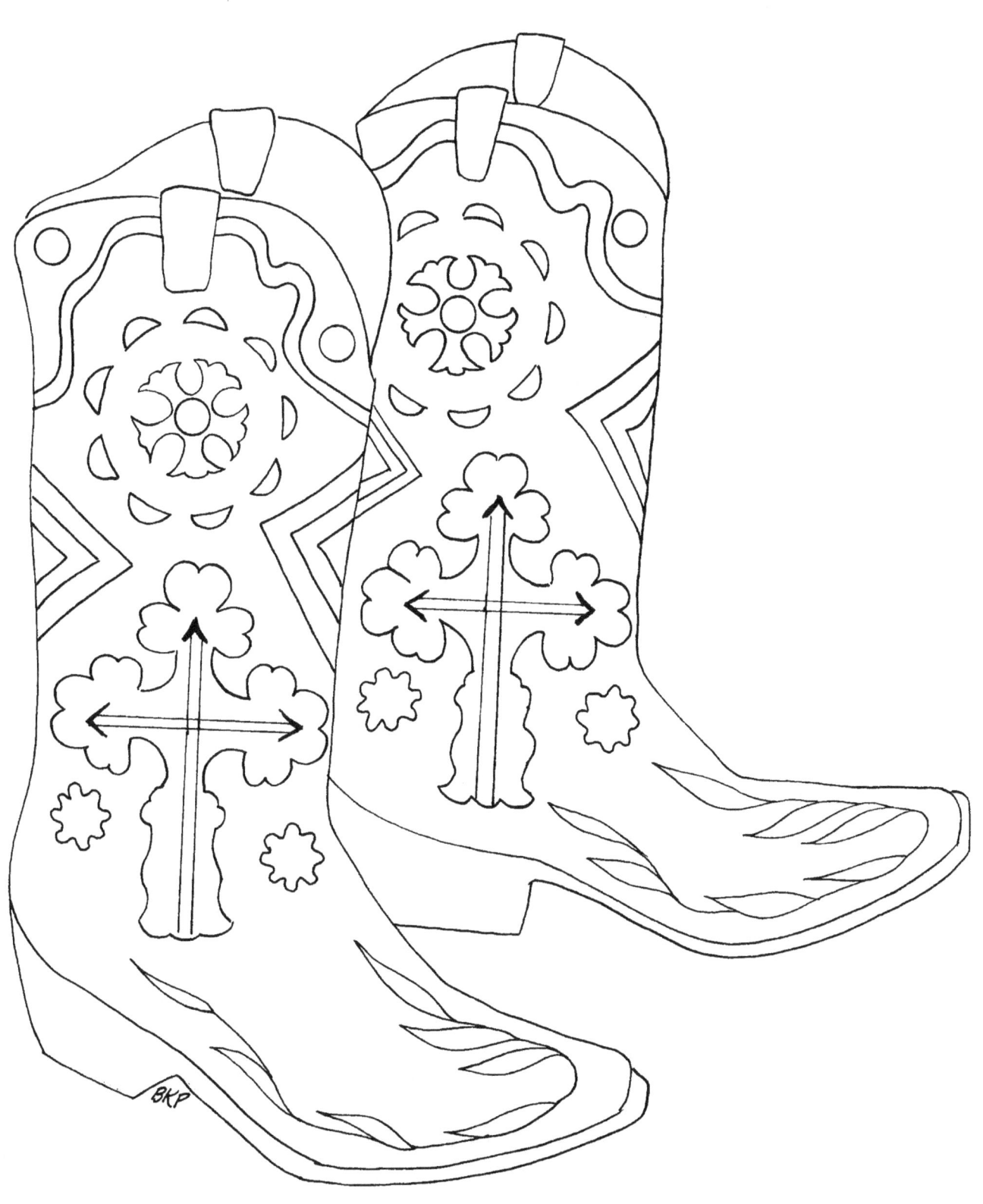

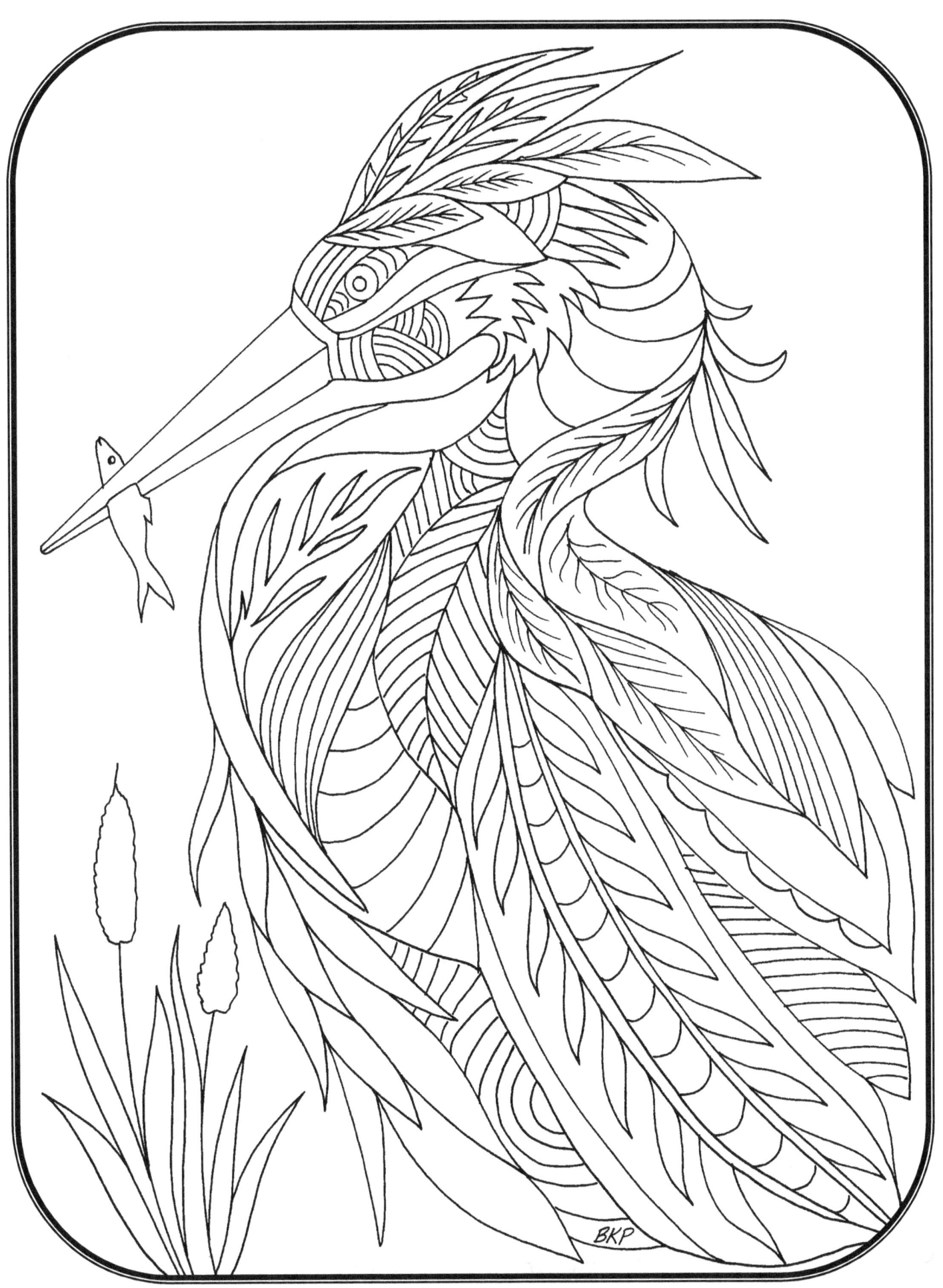

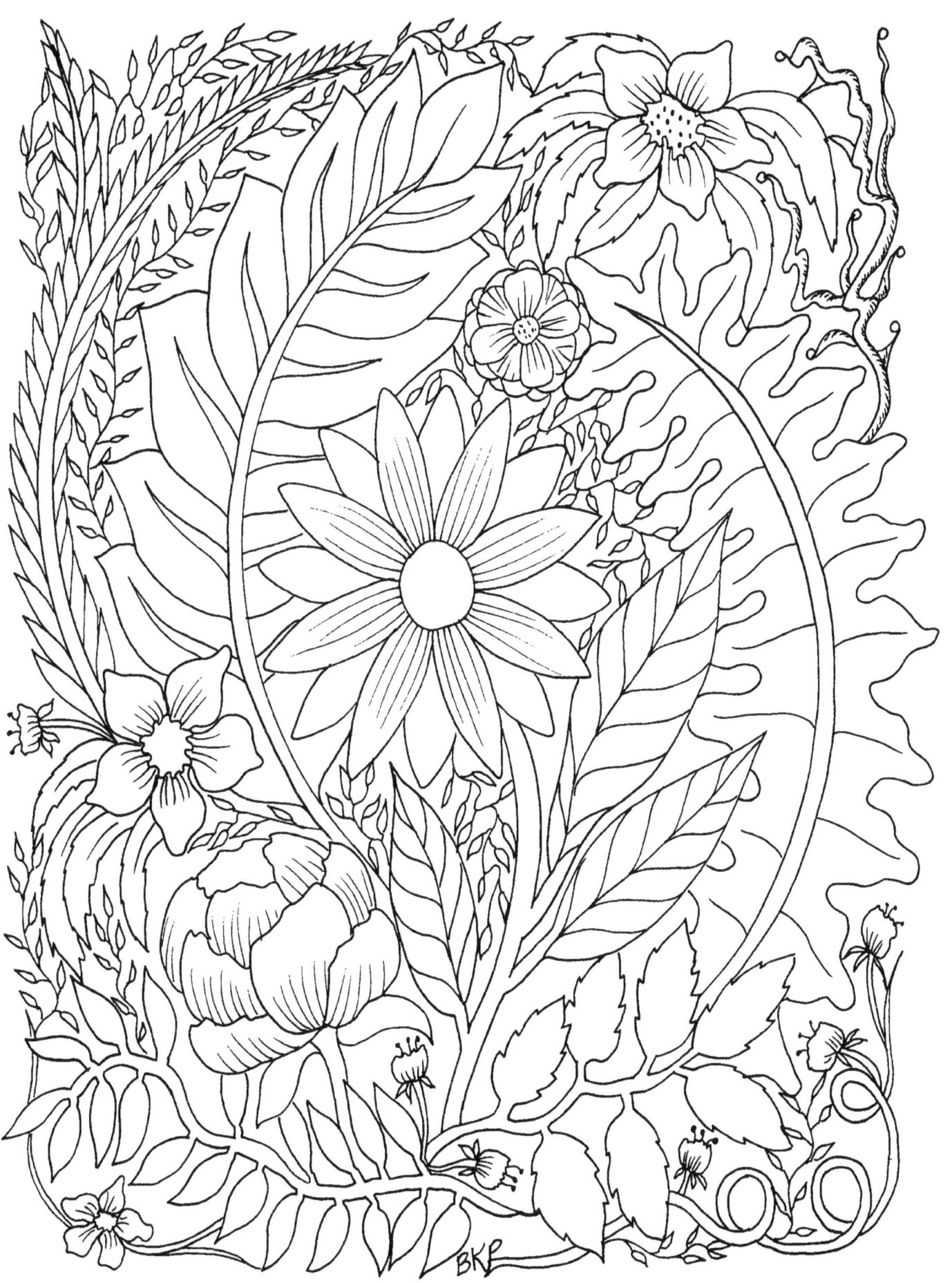

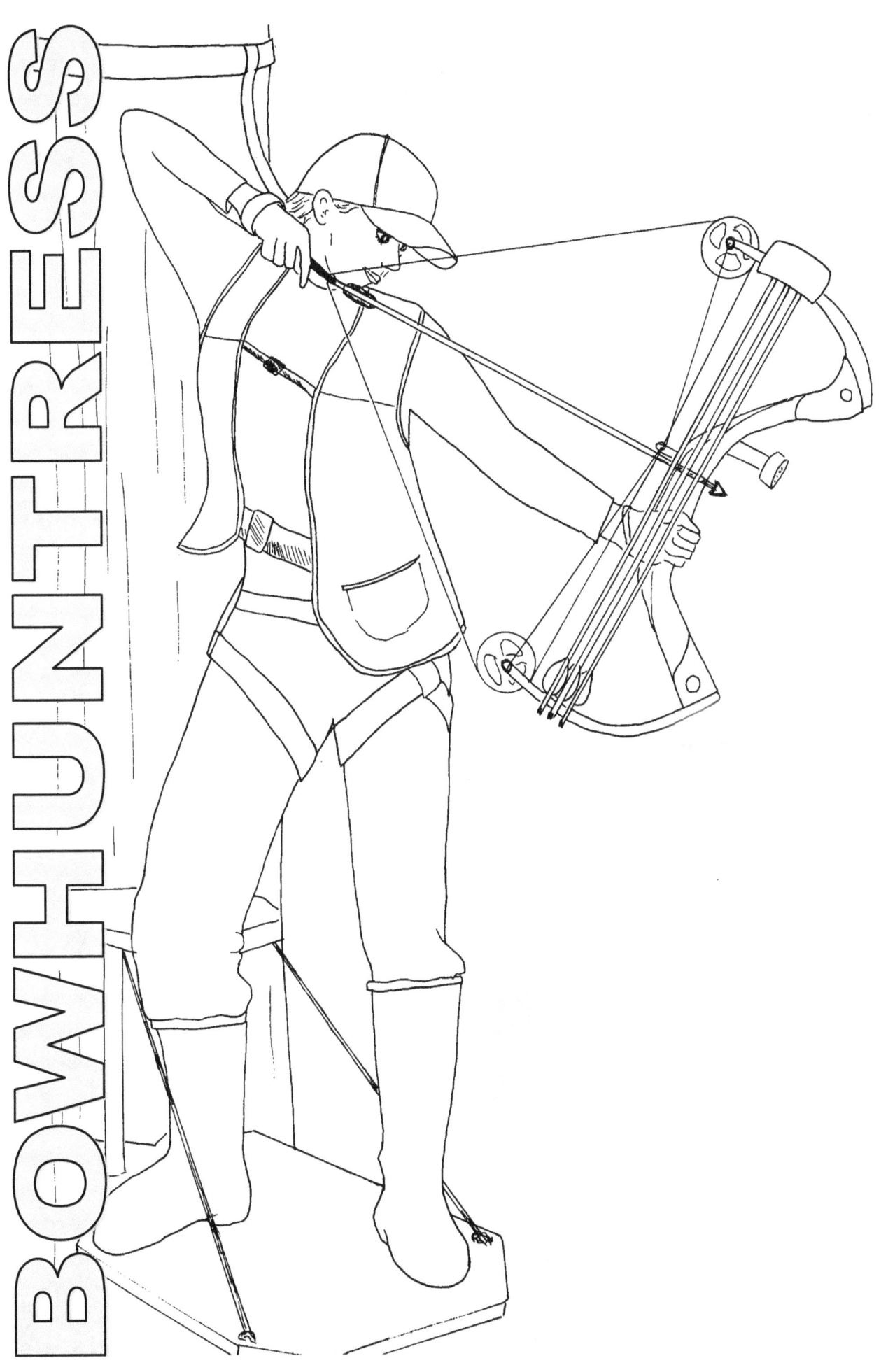

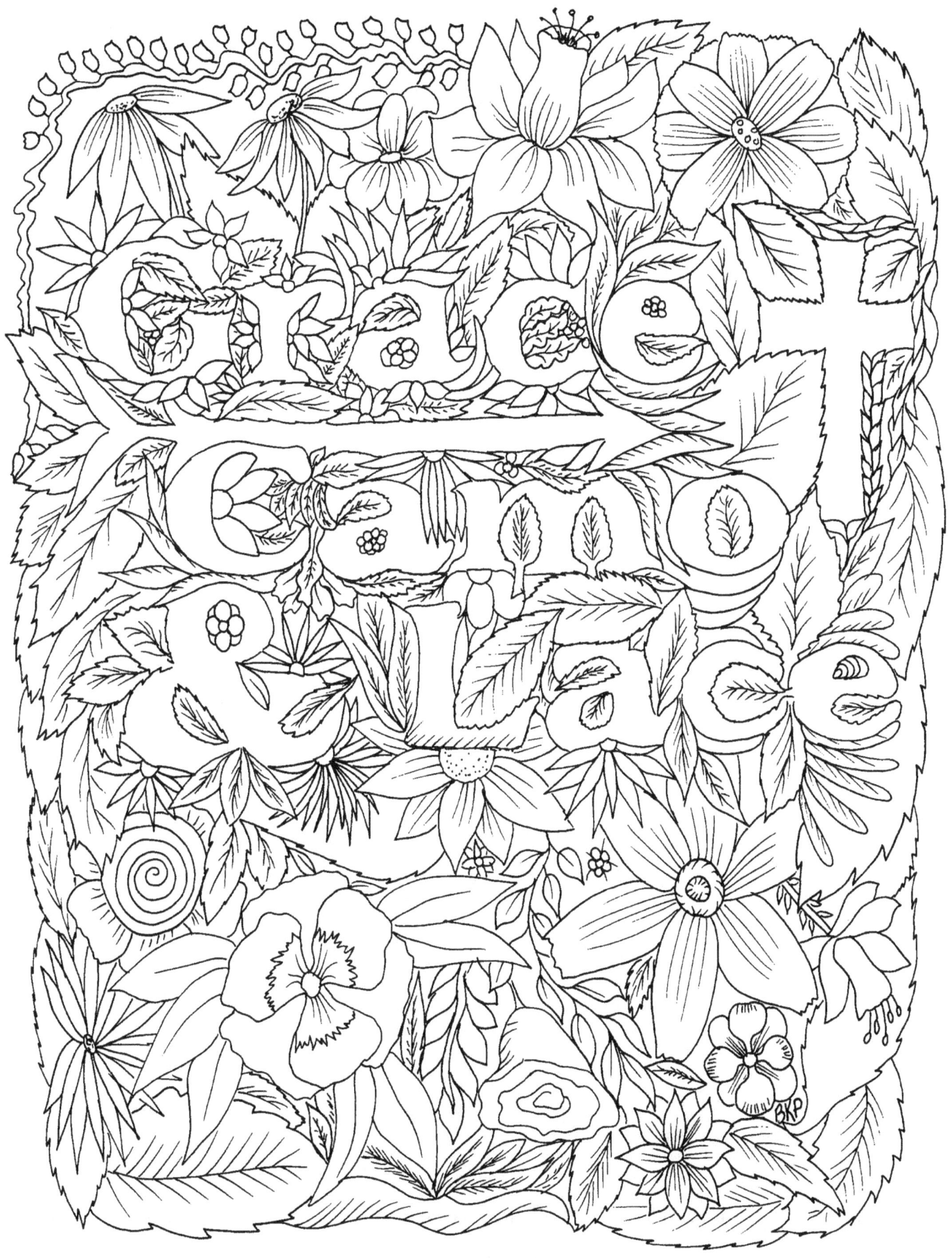

But we believe that through the grace of the Lord Jesus Christ we shall be saved, even as they.

Acts 15:11 KJV

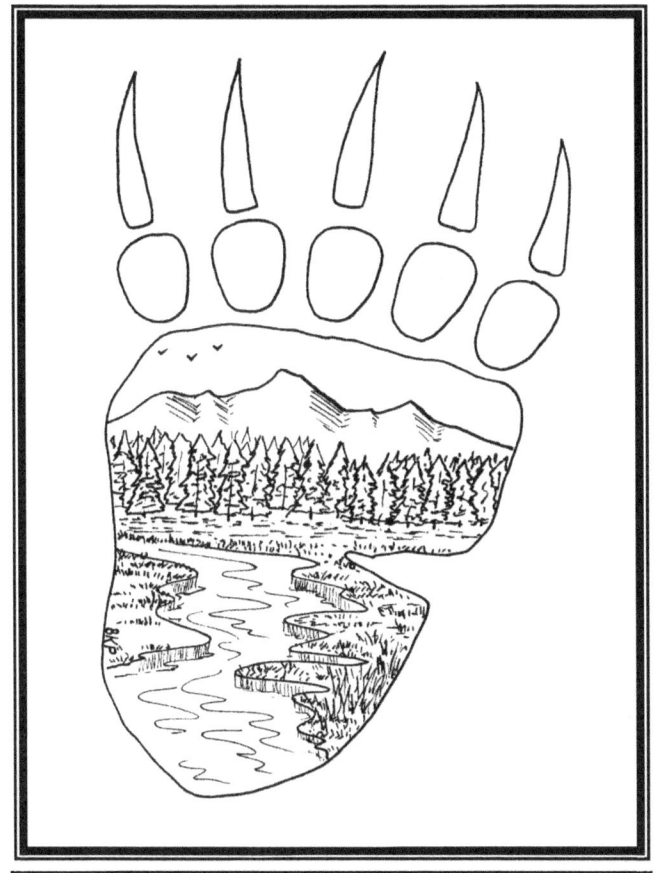

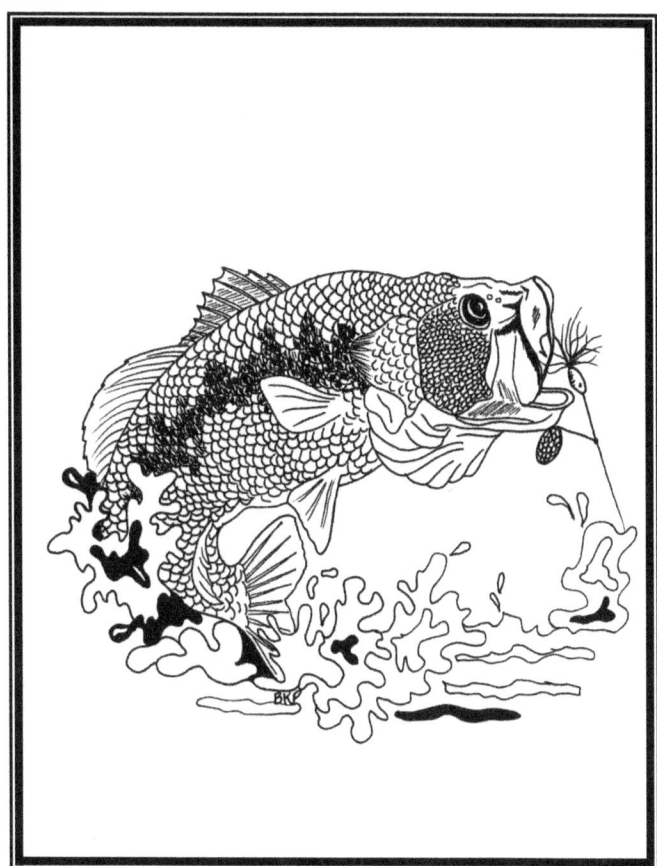

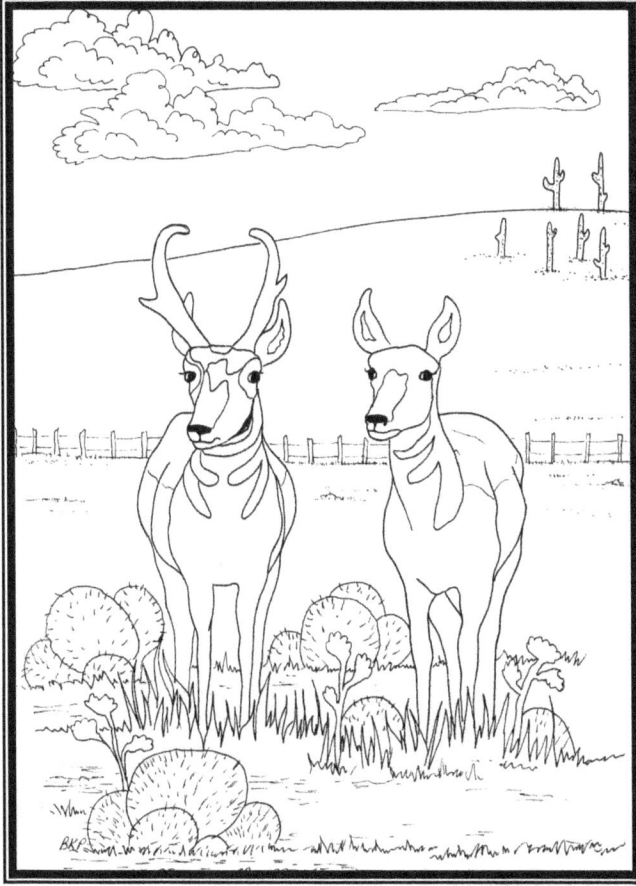

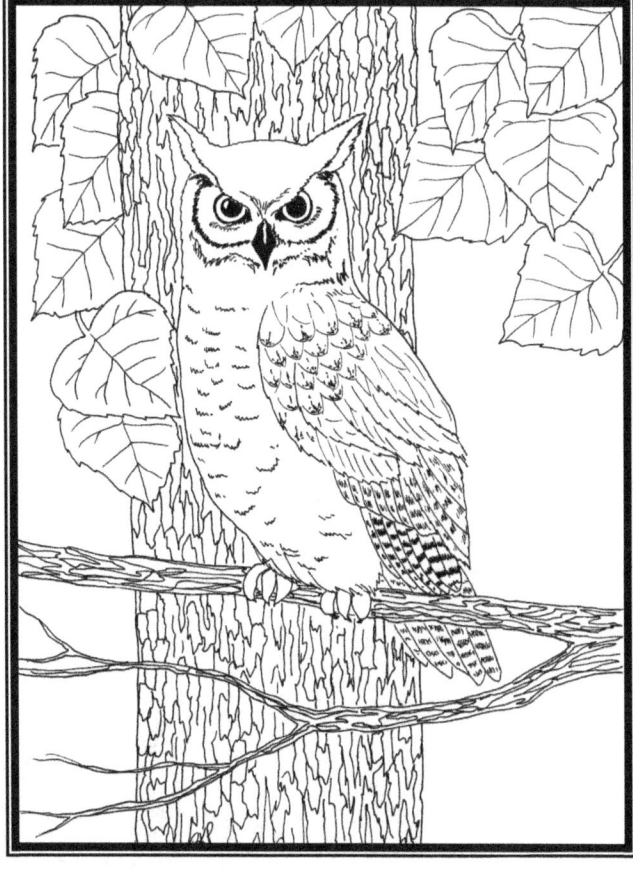